WORKS OF BERTOLT BRECHT

The Grove Press Edition

General Editor: Eric Bentley

Translators

Lee Baxandall

Eric Bentley

Martin Esslin

N. Goold-Verschoyle

H. R. Hays

Anselm Hollo

Christopher Isherwood

Frank Jones

Charles Laughton

Carl R. Mueller

Desmond I. Vesey

BERTOLT BRECHT

THE GOOD WOMAN
OF SETZUAN

Revised English version
and Introduction by
ERIC BENTLEY

GROVE PRESS, INC.   NEW YORK

ACKNOWLEDGMENT. The translator wishes to acknowledge the contribution of Mrs. Maja Apelman to the first version of the book *Parables of the Theatre,* as published by the University of Minnesota Press in 1948.

Library of Congress Catalog Card Number: 66-14106

First Evergreen Black Cat Edition 1966

MANUFACTURED IN THE UNITED STATES OF AMERICA

INTRODUCTION

Bertolt Brecht wrote *Der gute Mensch von Sezuan* in Scandinavia at the end of the nineteen-thirties. It was originally dedicated to his wife Helene Weigel, to whose playing it was ideally suited. Even the male part of the role would have been nothing new for her: she had played the Young Comrade in *The Measures Taken*. Yet, in fact, *The Good Woman* had its world première in Zurich during World War II, when Frau Weigel was a refugee in America. And by the time the play was produced by the Berliner Ensemble she was too old for the role. Meanwhile there had been many American productions.

In 1941 Brecht had crossed the USSR on the Trans-Siberian Railway and had then sailed across the Pacific to San Pedro, California. I was doing my first year of teaching at the time in the University of California at Los Angeles, and one of my students, who had got himself a hand printing press, wanted to print some poems. Another student said that a German poet was in town and had no translator. The name was Brecht—I was not aware of ever having heard it, though another writer on Brecht has pictured me listening to *Threepenny Opera* records as an undergraduate in the middle thirties. I arranged to see the poet with a view to translating several of his poems for my student's press.

Herr Brecht was living in a very small frame house in Santa Monica, and I was shown into his bedroom, which was also his study. He had few or no books. But there was a typewriter, and copies of *Freies Deutschland*—which I later found to be a Communist magazine published in Mexico—were strewn about. In the typewriter was the very thin paper, folded double, which I later knew to be characteristic of the man. It was on this paper—the kind used for carbon copies when you have no onionskin—that I first saw any of the work of Brecht. He handed me a couple of sheets of it while he looked over the samples of my own work I had brought along.

My impression of the man himself is hard to recapture at this distance in time. It is possible that I took Brecht for a truly proletarian writer on the score of his current lack of cash and his general style of living and dress. This would no doubt have been naive of me. Yet the charm and power of the encounter had their source in just this naïveté, and especially in the fact that I had no sense of being in the company of a famous man. Quite a contrast to those meetings with Brecht which young people were to have in the nineteen-fifties, when the cropped head and the tieless shirt were well known in advance from a score of photographs and a hundred anecdotes! For all I knew, Brecht might have had a trunkful of ties under the bed, and it could have been by chance that he was tieless at the time . . . or, as I say, it could have been because he was a "proletarian writer."

Most famous writers, of course, would have made sure that before I left after our first interview I did have a sense of their fame. Remarkable about Brecht was that he didn't bother about this. Here we see the real human value of what I came later to recognize as a certain deliberate depersonalization of things which Brecht brought about. He did not try to find out much about me. He did not invite me to find out much about him. As in his plays, two people would encounter each other for the sake of what they have to do together. I was a student of German and of poetry. He was a German and had written some poems. *I* would therefore translate some of *him*.

On the spot. And with his collaboration. For he already knew enough English to have a pretty shrewd idea whether a given expression corresponded to the German.

"Freilich, ich lebe in finsteren Zeiten!" That was the first line on one of the bits of tissue paper he had handed me. What did it mean? "Finstere Zeiten" are "dark ages." Was the reference to *the* Dark Ages? (I had no idea of the context.) "Nein, nein!" said the staccato voice. Then, after a puff at the cigar (not for me "the famous cigar"): "Nein, ich meine *diese* Zeiten, Herr Bentley, *unsere*—auch in Los Angeles kann es finster sein, nicht wahr?" He was teasing me a little. That, too, I would later regard as characteristic. At the time it was simply new. . . . Well, what about "freilich," what did one say in English for that? I suggested many things: "actually," "of course," "oh, yes," "it's true." To each one, the quiet yet sharp voice said: "Nein! Nein!" And Brecht shook his head very decisively. We were discovering together that in our effort to translate his poetry we could not get past the very first word.

The poetry, says Robert Frost, is the untranslatable part. This truth was empirically confirmed by Brecht and myself, but luckily it is a truth which all are agreed in advance to defy, and a half-truth at that. A lot of poetry just as problematical as Brecht's has come down to us in more languages than one—with whatever changes along the way. Although something must have happened to my student's hand press, for I never saw anything in print from it, I had begun translating Bertolt Brecht and am still doing so now, nearly a quarter of a century later.

For a while nothing was said about publication. But then Brecht wanted his poem "To the German Soldiers in the East" to come out. With him it was always a matter of the place and the time to publish something, considered not personally or "literarily," but politically: people in America should now read what he had to say about the German armies in Russia. So I translated that poem and sent it to *Partisan Review*. The choice was politically inept, since the editors were violently anti-Communist, but then, being anti-Communist, they knew about Brecht, which at that date other editors didn't. In fact, *Partisan* had run a "big" article about him in 1941. I was a little upset when Dwight MacDonald, rejecting the poem for the magazine, told me how outrageous he considered its contents to be. (In 1965 an editor of *Partisan* was to ask me please not to fight the Cold War when criticizing the Brecht theatre in East Berlin. Well, it is good that times change.) "To the German Soldiers in the East" finally appeared in Ray B. West's magazine, the *Rocky Mountain Review*.

Meanwhile, I had my first sizable assignment from Brecht: to translate, if not for cash on the line, at any rate for possible publication and performance, his full-length play *The Private Life of the Master Race*. This sequence of scenes about life under the Nazis had just been staged in German in New York City by Berthold Viertel, whom I had got to know, and it was Viertel who urged upon Brecht the possibility of an English-language production there, if a translation was on hand. By this time I was teaching at Black Mountain College in North Carolina, and the first performance of the English-language *Private Life* took place in the unlikely environment of the South. My students and I even broadcast a good deal of it on the Asheville radio. And when we did a staged reading of the whole play at the college, the composer Fritz Cohen performed at the organ. I recall a version of the Horst Wessel Song with magnificently distorted harmonies.

The plan to do the play in New York did not die but unfolded too slowly. The war was almost over when finally it was put on, and the public would not wish to hear another word about the Nazis for fifteen or twenty years. Also, the show itself was badly messed up. Brecht must have suspected from the beginning that it would be, for when he asked what the production outfit was called, and was told "The Theatre of All Nations," he had replied: "It's too many."

But Brecht publication in America had begun to get under way. Up to 1940 only the *Threepenny Novel* had been published, and that by a publisher whose interest in

Brecht was nonexistent. The first publisher to show real interest was Jay Laughlin, founder and owner of New Directions. He had brought out a translation of *Mother Courage* in 1941. He had *Private Life of the Master Race* ready in 1944. Around this time even warmer interest in Brecht was shown by the firm of Reynal and Hitchcock, and Brecht signed a contract with them for an edition of his collected works, of which I was to be general editor. How much happier, as well as simpler, the history of American Brecht publishing would have been had the plan gone through! But Curtice Hitchcock, whose brainchild it was, died soon after; the firm was sold to Harcourt, Brace; and Harcourt did not take over the Brecht project.

It proved impossible to interest any other publisher at that time in taking on the collected works of Brecht. Faced with this new situation, Brecht asked me to get individual plays published whenever opportunity offered and by whatever publishing house. Until 1960 I found only one publisher who would take on a volume of Brecht at all, and I got him published largely by the device of choosing his plays for inclusion in my own drama anthologies. Even this sometimes seemed eccentric to publishers. For example, at Doubleday's, when *Threepenny Opera* was included in my *Modern Theatre,* my editor-in-chief, Jason Epstein, who otherwise never objected to any of my choices, inquired: "What are we doing publishing an opera libretto?"

The one publisher to agree to bring out a volume of Brecht in these lean years was the University of Minnesota Press, which issued *Parables for the Theatre* in 1948. It cannot be said the publication created a sensation, or that the Press expected it to. But in the fifties Brecht caught on. *The Good Woman* and *Chalk Circle*—the two Parables of the Minnesota volume—were triumphantly produced in many countries, and Minnesota was able to lease paperback rights on their book to Grove Press in New York and London. Thereafter this became the best known of all Brecht books in English-speaking countries. And the two plays were performed far more than any of Brecht's others in British and American theatres.

The world première of *The Caucasian Chalk Circle* was at Carleton College, Northfield, Minnesota, in the spring of 1948. The same spring *The Good Woman* had its American première at Hamline University, St. Paul, Minnesota. All the more enterprising colleges then began doing the parables, and professional activity followed along at its lower rate of speed. I accepted an invitation to direct the first professional production of *The Caucasian Chalk Circle* at Hedgerow Theatre, near Philadelphia, in the summer of 1948. Meanwhile Uta Hagen had done a staged reading of *The Good Woman* in New York; she was later to play the title role in the first full production of the play in New York. Around 1950 *The Caucasian Chalk Circle* was among the small group of plays which brought together in Chicago the gifted people who would later be identified as members of "Second City" and "The Compass." (I well recall the struggle we had getting any royalties out of them.) Both the parables eventually became plays that all the more ambitious professional theatres knew they had to do. The Actor's Workshop of San Francisco offered a lavish production of *The Caucasian Chalk Circle* in 1963. The Minnesota Theatre Company in Minneapolis did the play at the Tyrone Guthrie Theatre in 1965.

A word about the text. It, too, has developed with the years. What Brecht said he wanted, for his first appearances in print in the United States, was a faithful word-for-word reproduction of the German. This he got, save for some errors which were caught later, in the first edition published by Minnesota. The only significant omission from the book at that time was that of the Prologue to *The Caucasian Chalk Circle*. For the manuscript was delivered to the publishers at about the time of Brecht's appearance before the House Un-American Activities Committee in Washington (October 1947). It was on advice from him that the appearance of this Prologue was postponed. From which incident have come two false rumors: one, that the Prologue was written later and so had not been part of Brecht's original draft of the play; two, that the omission was made on my initiative and so constituted editorial interference. It should be added that when an author says, "Let's not include such and such a passage till later," he may well not foresee *for how long* he is postponing its inclusion. To insert a prologue, the printer has to redo a whole play. The Prologue to *The Caucasian Chalk Circle*, though found in the German manuscript Brecht sent me in 1945, did not appear in English until the *Tulane Drama Review* printed it at my request in 1959. Soon thereafter, it turned up in the Grove Evergreen paperback edition of the play.

Perhaps all good foreign plays should be published first in a very literal translation and subsequently in various attempts at a true equivalent, even, if necessary, in "adaptations." Some plays can have high literary quality in another language and at the same time be fairly literal transcriptions. Others have not proved so amenable. (I put it thus cautiously to allow for the possibility that some or all of them might prove so amenable at some future time.) Brecht toyed with the idea of his plays always being literally translated for publication and freely adapted for performance. But even this is not a perfect formula. Whenever the stage version is more plausible, has more character, more charm, vivacity, edge, or whatnot, reasonable readers will prefer it not only in the theatre but in the study: for it is more readable. Hence, when I had to discard the literal translation of *The Good Woman* for stage purposes, the nonliteral text that resulted was adjudged preferable by publishers and readers as well as producers and spectators. For the Phoenix Theatre production (New York, 1956) I decided to ignore the literal translation altogether and, working again with the German, to make a completely new rendering for the stage. Since all the larger libraries have copies of the first Minnesota edition, anyone who is curious about this can look up for himself what the differences are. The 1956 text does amount to "adaptation" in the sense that some passages have not been translated at all but deliberately omitted or changed. Luckily, the author was still alive when these changes were proposed, and when I last saw Brecht (June 1956) he approved them in principle. (He was not interested in inspecting the script line by line and probably was not well enough to do so in any case.)

In English, things have to be said more tersely than in German. Hence, English translations from German should always come out shorter than the original. Sometimes that is a matter of phraseology only: each sentence should come out shorter. But at other times the very thought and substance of a German text has to be made more compact in English, and in this case whole sentences of the original have to go. Now once you start this more drastic kind of "cutting" you also find yourself obliged to bridge the "gaps" you have made with new writing. This is one of the ways in which translation becomes adaptation. . . . It did so in the reworking of *The Good Woman,* and those who wish to know exactly what Brecht said in every detail will, as I say, have to go to the German or the first Minnesota edition. Reprinted in this volume is the stage version used at the Phoenix, plus only the Epilogue which was not used in that show. (Since for a while Grove Press ran precisely the Phoenix text without the Epilogue, yet another false rumor circulated, and was exploited to compound the misunderstanding created by the rumor about the omitted Prologue to *Chalk Circle:* Brecht was *for the second time* being touched up by a translator hostile to Marxism. The coupling of the two rumors did not, of course, make sense, since the printings that omitted the Epilogue to *The Good Woman* contained the Prologue to *Chalk Circle.* Anyhow, the present editions contain both.)

For stage purposes, I found that everything in *The*

Good Woman had to be said more briefly and swiftly in English than in the German, and I think the reader too will appreciate a terser, lighter textured piece of reading matter. I would not make this identical statement about *The Caucasian Chalk Circle*. It is not an easier play to turn into English, but it is far less abstract and more poetic. Consequently, the obligation to keep each phrase is far greater, and the result of keeping each—or nearly each—phrase seems a gain, rather than a loss. This does not mean that as soon as one has written out an "accurate" translation one has finished work. There remains an endless labor, this time not of trimming, cutting, and reshaping scenes, but of weighing one word against another, one phrase against another, and, finally, of trying to achieve a style that might serve as *the* style of this play. The renewed work on *The Good Woman,* since the method meant going back to zero, seemed more radical and while it lasted was indeed more intensive, yet in the end even more work may have been put in on *Chalk Circle,* though this work was done a little at a time and was wholly a matter of details. (A work of art is an accumulation of details.) Many of the changes made in the English text of *Chalk Circle* were incorporated in the Grove Evergreen printings of the early sixties. Many others were first printed in the present edition. Of special use to me in the selection of new readings was the Harvard University production of the play (1960) directed by John Hancock.

One has always to ask of a Brecht translation what German text it is based on, since Brecht himself was forever changing what he wrote. The present English version is in principle based on the manuscript supplied by Brecht in 1945.* This fact explains one or two things that might otherwise appear anomalous. For example, "Sezuan"

---

* In the spring of 1946 Reynal and Hitchcock brought out my book *The Playwright as Thinker* in which Brecht's as yet unpublished "parables" were summarized.

was a city in the manuscript, though later it would be identified as "Szechwan," which is a province. Since Brecht obviously could not have had in mind a province when he wrote "a city," I consider the original reading sounder and have kept it. It is in line with all Brecht's other "misunderstandings" of geography and even with a stage tradition that goes back to things like the "seacoast of Bohemia" in Shakespeare. *Der kaukasische Kreidekreis* was published in substantially the form I knew it, not in the book editions, but in the 1949 Brecht Supplement of the magazine *Sinn und Form*. Since nothing in the English of *Chalk Circle* is in the nature of "free adaptation," the reader can be sure that if he finds any passage there that is not in the German text he consults it *is* taken from some other German text. For instance, the scabrous bit about the soldier getting an erection from stabbing was omitted from later German versions. Conversely, at Brecht's request, I inserted some rhymes to introduce the Azdak trial scenes which had not been found in the 1945 manuscript. To sum up: my rendering of *Chalk Circle* claims to provide a line by line equivalent of the German, though "the German" is itself a flexible term in this context; while *The Good Woman* adheres far less closely to *Der gute Mensch von Sezuan*, which, however, readers can find translated literally in the first Minnesota edition.

—E. B.

Berlin, March 1965

THE GOOD WOMAN
OF SETZUAN

CHARACTERS

Wong, *a water seller*

Three Gods

Shen Te, *a prostitute, later a shopkeeper*

Mrs. Shin, *former owner of Shen Te's shop*

A Family of Eight (*husband, wife, brother, sister-in-law, grandfather, nephew, niece, boy*)

An Unemployed Man

A Carpenter

Mrs. Mi Tzu, *Shen Te's landlady*

Yang Sun, *an unemployed pilot, later a factory manager*

An Old Whore

A Policeman

An Old Man

An Old Woman, *his wife*

Mr. Shu Fu, *a barber*

Mrs. Yang, *mother of Yang Sun*

Gentlemen, Voices, Children (*three*), *etc.*

PROLOGUE

At the gates of the half-Westernized city of Setzuan. Evening. WONG *the water seller introduces himself to the audience.*

WONG: I sell water here in the city of Setzuan. It isn't easy. When water is scarce, I have long distances to go in search of it, and when it is plentiful, I have no income. But in our part of the world there is nothing unusual about poverty. Many people think only the gods can save the situation. And I hear from a cattle merchant—who travels a lot—that some of the highest gods are on their way here at this very moment. Informed sources have it that heaven is quite disturbed at all the complaining. I've been coming out here to the city gates for three days now to bid these gods welcome. I want to be the first to greet them. What about those fellows over there? No, no, they *work*. And that one there has ink on his fingers, he's no god, he must be a clerk from the cement factory. *Those* two are another story. They look as though they'd like to beat you. But gods don't need to beat you, do they?

THREE GODS *appear.*

What about those three? Old-fashioned clothes—dust on their feet—they *must* be gods! (*He throws himself at their feet.*) Do with me what you will, illustrious ones!

FIRST GOD (*with an ear trumpet*): Ah! (*He is pleased.*) So we were expected?

17

WONG (*giving them water*): Oh, yes. And I *knew* you'd come.

FIRST GOD: We need somewhere to stay the night. You know of a place?

WONG: The whole town is at your service, illustrious ones! What sort of a place would you like?

The GODS *eye each other.*

FIRST GOD: Just try the first house you come to, my son.

WONG: That would be Mr. Fo's place.

FIRST GOD: Mr. Fo.

WONG: One moment! (*He knocks at the first house.*)

VOICE FROM MR. FO'S: No!

WONG *returns a little nervously.*

WONG: It's too bad. Mr. Fo isn't in. And his servants don't dare do a thing without his consent. He'll have a fit when he finds out who they turned away, won't he?

FIRST GOD (*smiling*): He will, won't he?

WONG: One moment! The next house is Mr. Cheng's. Won't he be thrilled!

FIRST GOD: Mr. Cheng.

WONG *knocks.*

VOICE FROM MR. CHENG'S: Keep your gods. We have our own troubles!

WONG (*back with the* GODS): Mr. Cheng is very sorry, but he has a houseful of relations. I think some of them are a bad lot, and naturally, he wouldn't like you to see them.

THIRD GOD: Are we so terrible?

WONG: Well, only with bad people, of course. Everyone knows the province of Kwan is always having floods.

SECOND GOD: Really? How's that?

WONG: Why, because they're so irreligious.

SECOND GOD: Rubbish. It's because they neglected the dam.

FIRST GOD (*to* SECOND): Sh! (*To* WONG:) You're still in hopes, aren't you, my son?

WONG: Certainly. All Setzuan is competing for the honor! What happened up to now is pure coincidence. I'll be back. (*He walks away, but then stands undecided.*)

SECOND GOD: What did I tell you?

THIRD GOD: It *could* be pure coincidence.

SECOND GOD: The same coincidence in Shun, Kwan, and Setzuan? People just aren't religious any more, let's face the fact. Our mission has failed!

FIRST GOD: Oh come, we might run into a good person any minute.

THIRD GOD: How did the resolution read? (*Unrolling a scroll and reading from it*:) "The world can stay as it is if enough people are found (*at the word "found" he unrolls it a little more*) living lives worthy of human beings." Good people, that is. Well, what about this water seller himself? *He's* good, or I'm very much mistaken.

SECOND GOD: You're very much mistaken. When he gave us a drink, I had the impression there was something odd about the cup. Well, look! (*He shows the cup to the* FIRST GOD.)

FIRST GOD: A false bottom!

SECOND GOD: The man is a swindler.

FIRST GOD: Very well, count *him* out. That's one man among millions. And as a matter of fact, we only need one on *our* side. These atheists are saying, "The world must be changed because no one can *be* good and *stay* good." No one, eh? I say: let us find one—just one—and we have those fellows where we want them!

THIRD GOD (*to* WONG): Water seller, is it so hard to find a place to stay?

WONG: Nothing could be easier. It's just me. I don't go about it right.

THIRD GOD: Really?

He returns to the others. A GENTLEMAN *passes by.*

WONG: Oh dear, they're catching on. (*He accosts the* GENTLEMAN.) Excuse the intrusion, dear sir, but three gods have just turned up. Three of the very highest. They need a place for the night. Seize this rare opportunity—to have real gods as your guests!

GENTLEMAN (*laughing*): A new way of finding free rooms for a gang of crooks. (*Exit* GENTLEMAN.)

WONG (*shouting at him*): Godless rascal! Have you no religion, gentleman of Setzuan? (*Pause.*) Patience, illustrious ones! (*Pause.*) There's only one person left. Shen Te, the prostitute. She *can't* say no. (*Calls up to a window:*) Shen Te!

SHEN TE *opens the shutters and looks out.*

WONG: Shen Te, it's Wong. *They're* here, and nobody wants them. Will you take them?

SHEN TE: Oh, no, Wong, I'm expecting a gentleman.

WONG: Can't you forget about him for tonight?

SHEN TE: The rent has to be paid by tomorrow or I'll be out on the street.

WONG: This is no time for calculation, Shen Te.

SHEN TE: Stomachs rumble even on the Emperor's birthday, Wong.

WONG: Setzuan is one big dung hill!

SHEN TE: Oh, very well! I'll hide till my gentleman has come and gone. Then I'll take them. (*She disappears.*)

WONG: They mustn't see her gentleman or they'll know what she is.

FIRST GOD (*who hasn't heard any of this*): I think it's hopeless.

They approach WONG.

WONG (*jumping, as he finds them behind him*): A room has been found, illustrious ones! (*He wipes sweat off his brow.*)

SECOND GOD: Oh, good.

THIRD GOD: Let's see it.

WONG (*nervously*): Just a minute. It has to be tidied up a bit.

THIRD GOD: Then we'll sit down here and wait.

WONG (*still more nervous*): No, no! (*Holding himself back.*) Too much traffic, you know.

THIRD GOD (*with a smile*): Of course, if you *want* us to move.

They retire a little. They sit on a doorstep. WONG *sits on the ground.*

WONG (*after a deep breath*): You'll be staying with a single girl—the finest human being in Setzuan!

THIRD GOD: That's nice.

WONG (*to the audience*): They gave me such a look when I picked up my cup just now.

THIRD GOD: You're worn out, Wong.

WONG: A little, maybe.

FIRST GOD: Do people here have a hard time of it?

WONG: The good ones do.

FIRST GOD: What about yourself?

WONG: You mean I'm not good. That's true. And I don't have an easy time either!

During this dialogue, a GENTLEMAN *has turned up*

in front of Shen Te's house, and has whistled several times. Each time WONG *has given a start.*

THIRD GOD (*to* WONG, *softly*): Psst! I think he's gone now.

WONG (*confused and surprised*): Ye-e-es.

The GENTLEMAN *has left now, and* SHEN TE *has come down to the street.*

SHEN TE (*softly*): Wong!

Getting no answer, she goes off down the street. WONG *arrives just too late, forgetting his carrying pole.*

WONG (*softly*): Shen Te! Shen Te! (*To himself:*) So she's gone off to earn the rent. Oh dear, I can't go to the gods *again* with no room to offer them. Having failed in the service of the gods, I shall run to my den in the sewer pipe down by the river and hide from their sight!

He rushes off. SHEN TE *returns, looking for him, but finding the* GODS. *She stops in confusion.*

SHEN TE: You are the illustrious ones? My name is Shen Te. It would please me very much if my simple room could be of use to you.

THIRD GOD: Where is the water seller, Miss . . . Shen Te?

SHEN TE: I missed him, somehow.

FIRST GOD: Oh, he probably thought you weren't coming, and was afraid of telling us.

THIRD GOD (*picking up the carrying pole*): We'll leave this with you. He'll be needing it.

Led by SHEN TE, *they go into the house. It grows dark, then light. Dawn. Again escorted by* SHEN TE, *who leads them through the half-light with a little lamp, the* GODS *take their leave.*

FIRST GOD: Thank you, thank you, dear Shen Te, for your elegant hospitality! We shall not forget! And give our thanks to the water seller—he showed us a good human being.

SHEN TE: Oh, *I'm* not good. Let me tell you something: when Wong asked me to put you up, I hesitated.

FIRST GOD: It's all right to hesitate if you then go ahead! And in giving us that room you did much more that you knew. You proved that good people still exist, a point that has been disputed of late—even in heaven. Farewell!

SECOND GOD: Farewell!

THIRD GOD: Farewell!

SHEN TE: Stop, illustrious ones! I'm not sure you're right. I'd like to be good, it's true, but there's the rent to pay. And that's not all: I sell myself for a living. Even so I can't make ends meet, there's too much competition. I'd like to honor my father and mother and speak nothing but the truth and not covet my neighbor's house. I should love to stay with one man. But how? How is it done? Even breaking a few of your commandments, I can hardly manage.

FIRST GOD (*clearing his throat*): These thoughts are but, um, the misgivings of an unusually good woman!

THIRD GOD: Good-bye, Shen Te! Give our regards to the water seller!

SECOND GOD: And above all: be good! Farewell!

FIRST GOD: Farewell!

THIRD GOD: Farewell!

They start to wave good-bye.

SHEN TE: But everything is so expensive, I don't feel sure I can do it!

SECOND GOD: That's not in our sphere. We never meddle with economics.

THIRD GOD: One moment. (*They stop.*) Isn't it true she might do better if she had more money?

SECOND GOD: Come, come! How could we ever account for it Up Above?

FIRST GOD: Oh, there are ways. (*They put their heads together and confer in dumb show. To* SHEN TE, *with embarrassment:*) As you say you can't pay your rent, well, um, we're not paupers, so of course we *insist* on paying for our room. (*Awkwardly thrusting money into her hand.*) There! (*Quickly.*) But don't tell anyone! The incident is open to misinterpretation.

SECOND GOD: It certainly is!

FIRST GOD (*defensively*): But there's no law against it! It was never decreed that a god mustn't pay hotel bills!

The GODS *leave.*

1

*A small tobacco shop. The shop is not as yet completely
furnished and hasn't started doing business.*

SHEN TE (*to the audience*): It's three days now since the
   gods left. When they said they wanted to pay for the
   room, I looked down at my hand, and there was
   more than a thousand silver dollars! I bought a
   tobacco shop with the money, and moved in yesterday. I don't own the building, of course, but I can
   pay the rent, and I hope to do a lot of good here.
   Beginning with Mrs. Shin, who's just coming across
   the square with her pot. She had the shop before
   me, and yesterday she dropped in to ask for rice
   for her children. (*Enter* MRS. SHIN. *Both women
   bow.*) How do you do, Mrs. Shin.

MRS. SHIN: How do you do, Miss Shen Te. You like your
   new home?

SHEN TE: Indeed, yes. Did your children have a good
   night?

MRS. SHIN: In that hovel? The youngest is coughing
   already.

SHEN TE: Oh, dear!

MRS. SHIN: You're going to learn a thing or two in these
   slums.

SHEN TE: Slums? That's not what you said when you sold
   me the shop!

26

MRS. SHIN: Now don't start nagging! Robbing me and my innocent children of their home and then calling it a slum! That's the limit! (*She weeps.*)

SHEN TE (*tactfully*): I'll get your rice.

MRS. SHIN: And a little cash while you're at it.

SHEN TE: I'm afraid I haven't sold anything yet.

MRS. SHIN (*screeching*): I've got to have it. Strip the clothes from my back and then cut my throat, will you? I know what I'll do: I'll dump my children on your doorstep! (*She snatches the pot out of* SHEN TE'*s hands.*)

SHEN TE: Please don't be angry. You'll spill the rice.

Enter an elderly HUSBAND *and* WIFE *with their shabbily dressed* NEPHEW.

WIFE: Shen Te, dear! You've come into money, they tell me. And we haven't a roof over our heads! A tobacco shop. We had one too. But it's gone. Could we spend the night here, do you think?

NEPHEW (*appraising the shop*): Not bad!

WIFE: He's our nephew. We're inseparable!

MRS. SHIN: And who are these . . . ladies and gentlemen?

SHEN TE: They put me up when I first came in from the country. (*To the audience:*) Of course, when my small purse was empty, they put me out on the street, and they may be afraid I'll do the same to them. (*To the newcomers, kindly:*) Come in, and welcome, though I've only one little room for you— it's behind the shop.

HUSBAND: That'll do. Don't worry.

WIFE (*bringing* SHEN TE *some tea*): We'll stay over here, so we won't be in your way. Did you make it a tobacco shop in memory of your first real home? We can certainly give you a hint or two! That's one reason we came.

MRS. SHIN (*to* SHEN TE): Very nice! As long as you have a few customers too!

HUSBAND: Sh! A customer!

Enter an UNEMPLOYED MAN, *in rags.*

UNEMPLOYED MAN: Excuse me. I'm unemployed.

MRS. SHIN *laughs.*

SHEN TE: Can I help you?

UNEMPLOYED MAN: Have you any damaged cigarettes? I thought there might be some damage when you're unpacking.

WIFE: What nerve, begging for tobacco! (*Rhetorically.*) Why don't they ask for bread?

UNEMPLOYED MAN: Bread is expensive. One cigarette butt and I'll be a new man.

SHEN TE (*giving him cigarettes*): That's very important —to be a new man. You'll be my first customer and bring me luck.

The UNEMPLOYED MAN *quickly lights a cigarette, inhales, and goes off, coughing.*

WIFE: Was that right, Shen Te, dear?

MRS. SHIN: If this is the opening of a shop, you can hold the closing at the end of the week.

HUSBAND: I bet he had money on him.

SHEN TE: Oh, no, he said he hadn't!

NEPHEW: How d'you know he wasn't lying?

SHEN TE (*angrily*): How do you know he was?

WIFE (*wagging her head*): You're too good, Shen Te, dear. If you're going to keep this shop, you'll have to learn to say no.

HUSBAND: Tell them the place isn't yours to dispose of. Belongs to . . . some relative who insists on all accounts being strictly in order . . .

MRS. SHIN: That's right! What do you think you are—a philanthropist?

SHEN TE (*laughing*): Very well, suppose I ask you for my rice back, Mrs. Shin?

WIFE (*combatively, at* MRS. SHIN): So that's *her* rice?

Enter the CARPENTER, *a small man.*

MRS. SHIN (*who, at the sight of him, starts to hurry away*): See you tomorrow, Miss Shen Te! (*Exit* MRS. SHIN.)

CARPENTER: Mrs. Shin, it's you I want!

WIFE (*to* SHEN TE): Has she some claim on you?

SHEN TE: She's hungry. That's a claim.

CARPENTER: Are you the new tenant? And filling up the shelves already? Well, they're not yours till they're paid for, ma'am. I'm the carpenter, so I should know.

SHEN TE: I took the shop "furnishings included."

CARPENTER: You're in league with that Mrs. Shin, of course. All right. I demand my hundred silver dollars.

SHEN TE: I'm afraid I haven't got a hundred silver dollars.

CARPENTER: Then you'll find it. Or I'll have you arrested.

WIFE (*whispering to* SHEN TE): That relative: make it a cousin.

SHEN TE: Can't it wait till next month?

CARPENTER: No!

SHEN TE: Be a little patient, Mr. Carpenter, I can't settle all claims at once.

CARPENTER: Who's patient with me? (*He grabs a shelf from the wall.*) Pay up—or I take the shelves back!

WIFE: Shen Te! Dear! Why don't you let your . . . cousin settle this affair? (*To* CARPENTER:) Put your claim in writing. Shen Te's cousin will see you get paid.

CARPENTER (*derisively*): Cousin, eh?

HUSBAND: Cousin, yes.

CARPENTER: I know these cousins!

NEPHEW: Don't be silly. He's a personal friend of mine.

HUSBAND: What a man! Sharp as a razor!

CARPENTER: All right. I'll put my claim in writing. (*Puts shelf on floor, sits on it, writes out bill.*)

WIFE (*to* SHEN TE): He'd tear the dress off your back to get his shelves. Never recognize a claim. That's my motto.

SHEN TE: He's done a job, and wants something in return. It's shameful that I can't give it to him. What will the gods say?

HUSBAND: You did your bit when you took *us* in.

Enter the BROTHER, *limping, and the* SISTER-IN-LAW, *pregnant.*

BROTHER (*to* HUSBAND *and* WIFE): So this is where you're hiding out! There's family feeling for you! Leaving us on the corner!

WIFE (*embarrassed, to* SHEN TE): It's my brother and his wife. (*To them:*) Now stop grumbling, and sit quietly in that corner. (*To* SHEN TE:) It can't be helped. She's in her fifth month.

SHEN TE: Oh yes. Welcome!

WIFE (*to the couple*): Say thank you. (*They mutter something.*) The cups are there. (*To* SHEN TE:) Lucky you bought this shop when you did!

SHEN TE (*laughing and bringing tea*): Lucky indeed!

Enter MRS. MI TZU, *the landlady.*

MRS. MI TZU: Miss Shen Te? I am Mrs. Mi Tzu, your landlady. I hope our relationship will be a happy one. I like to think I give my tenants modern, personalized service. Here is your lease. (*To the others, as* SHEN TE *reads the lease*:) There's nothing like the opening of a little shop, is there? A moment of true beauty! (*She is looking around.*) Not very much on the shelves, of course. But everything in the gods' good time! Where are your references, Miss Shen Te?

SHEN TE: Do I *have* to have references?

MRS. MI TZU: After all, I haven't a notion who you are!

HUSBAND: Oh, *we'd* be glad to vouch for Miss Shen Te! We'd go through fire for her!

MRS. MI TZU: And who may *you* be?

HUSBAND (*stammering*): Ma Fu, tobacco dealer.

MRS. MI TZU: Where is your shop, Mr. . . . Ma Fu?

HUSBAND: Well, um, I haven't got a shop—I've just sold it.

MRS. MI TZU: I see. (*To* SHEN TE:) Is there no one else that knows you?

WIFE (*whispering to* SHEN TE): Your cousin! Your cousin!

MRS. MI TZU: This is a respectable house, Miss Shen Te. I never sign a lease without certain assurances.

SHEN TE (*slowly, her eyes downcast*): I have . . . a cousin.

MRS. MI TZU: On the square? Let's go over and see him. What does he do?

SHEN TE (*as before*): He lives . . . in another city.

WIFE (*prompting*): Didn't you say he was in Shung?

SHEN TE: That's right. Shung.

HUSBAND (*prompting*): I had his name on the tip of my tongue. Mr. . . .

SHEN TE (*with an effort*): Mr. . . . Shui . . . Ta.

HUSBAND: That's it! Tall, skinny fellow!

SHEN TE: Shui Ta!

NEPHEW (*to* CARPENTER): *You* were in touch with him, weren't you? About the shelves?

CARPENTER (*surlily*): Give him this bill. (*He hands it over.*) I'll be back in the morning. (*Exit* CARPENTER.)

NEPHEW (*calling after him, but with his eyes on* MRS. MI TZU): Don't worry! Mr. Shui Ta pays on the nail!

MRS. MI TZU (*looking closely at* SHEN TE): I'll be happy to make his acquaintance, Miss Shen Te. (*Exit* MRS. MI TZU.)

Pause.

WIFE: By tomorrow morning she'll know more about you than you do yourself.

SISTER-IN-LAW (*to* NEPHEW): This thing isn't built to last.

Enter GRANDFATHER.

WIFE: It's Grandfather! (*To* SHEN TE:) Such a good old soul!

The BOY *enters.*

BOY (*over his shoulder*): Here they are!

WIFE: And the boy, how he's grown! But he always could eat enough for ten.

Enter the NIECE.

WIFE (*to* SHEN TE): Our little niece from the country. There are more of us now than in your time. The less we had, the more there were of us; the more there were of us, the less we had. Give me the key. We must protect ourselves from unwanted guests. (*She takes the key and locks the door.*) Just make yourself at home. I'll light the little lamp.

NEPHEW (*a big joke*): I hope her cousin doesn't drop in tonight! The strict Mr. Shui Ta!

SISTER-IN-LAW *laughs.*

BROTHER (*reaching for a cigarette*): One cigarette more or less . . .

HUSBAND: One cigarette more or less.

They pile into the cigarettes. The BROTHER *hands a jug of wine round.*

NEPHEW: Mr. Shui Ta'll pay for it!

GRANDFATHER (*gravely, to* SHEN TE): How do you do?

SHEN TE, *a little taken aback by the belatedness of the greeting, bows. She has the carpenter's bill in one hand, the landlady's lease in the other.*

WIFE: How about a bit of a song? To keep Shen Te's spirits up?

NEPHEW: Good idea. Grandfather: you start!

SONG OF THE SMOKE

GRANDFATHER:

> I used to think (before old age beset me)
>> That brains could fill the pantry of the poor.
>
> But where did all my cerebration get me?
>> I'm just as hungry as I was before.
>>> So what's the use?
>>> See the smoke float free
>>> Into ever colder coldness!
>>> It's the same with me.

HUSBAND:

> The straight and narrow path leads to disaster
>> And so the crooked path I tried to tread.
>
> That got me to disaster even faster.
>> (They say we shall be happy when we're dead.)
>>> So what's the use?
>>> See the smoke float free
>>> Into ever colder coldness!
>>> It's the same with me.

NIECE:

> You older people, full of expectation,
>> At any moment now you'll walk the plank!
>
> The future's for the younger generation!
>> Yes, even if that future is a blank.
>>> So what's the use?
>>> See the smoke float free
>>> Into ever colder coldness!
>>> It's the same with me.

NEPHEW (*to the* BROTHER): Where'd you get that wine?

SISTER-IN-LAW (*answering for the* BROTHER): He pawned the sack of tobacco.

HUSBAND (*stepping in*): What? That tobacco was all we had to fall back on! You pig!

BROTHER: *You'd* call a man a pig because your wife was frigid! Did you refuse to drink it?

They fight. The shelves fall over.

SHEN TE (*imploringly*): Oh don't! Don't break everything! Take it, take it, take it all, but don't destroy a gift from the gods!

WIFE (*disparagingly*): This shop isn't big enough. I should never have mentioned it to Uncle and the others. When *they* arrive, it's going to be disgustingly over-crowded.

SISTER-IN-LAW: And did you hear our gracious hostess? She cools off quick!

Voices outside. Knocking at the door.

UNCLE'S VOICE: Open the door!

WIFE: Uncle! Is that you, Uncle?

UNCLE'S VOICE: Certainly, it's me. Auntie says to tell you she'll have the children here in ten minutes.

WIFE (*to* SHEN TE): I'll have to let him in.

SHEN TE (*who scarcely hears her*):
The little lifeboat is swiftly sent down
Too many men too greedily
Hold on to it as they drown.

1a

Wong's den in a sewer pipe.

WONG (*crouching there*): All quiet! It's four days now since I left the city. The gods passed this way on the second day. I heard their steps on the bridge over there. They must be a long way off by this time, so I'm safe. (*Breathing a sigh of relief, he curls up and goes to sleep. In his dream the pipe becomes transparent, and the* GODS *appear. Raising an arm, as if in self-defense*:) I know, I know, illustrious ones! I found no one to give you a room—not in all Setzuan! There, it's out. Please continue on your way!

FIRST GOD (*mildly*): But you did find someone. Someone who took us in for the night, watched over us in our sleep, and in the early morning lighted us down to the street with a lamp.

WONG: It was . . . Shen Te that took you in?

THIRD GOD: Who else?

WONG: And I ran away! "She isn't coming," I thought, "she just can't afford it."

GODS (*singing*):
O you feeble, well-intentioned, and yet feeble chap
Where there's need the fellow thinks there is
    no goodness!
When there's danger he thinks courage starts to
    ebb away!

Some people only see the seamy side!
What hasty judgment! What premature desperation!

WONG: I'm *very* ashamed, illustrious ones.

FIRST GOD: Do us a favor, water seller. Go back to Setzuan. Find Shen Te, and give us a report on her. We hear that she's come into a little money. Show interest in her goodness—for no one can be good for long if goodness is not in demand. Meanwhile we shall continue the search, and find other good people. After which, the idle chatter about the impossibility of goodness will stop!

The GODS vanish.

2

A knocking.

WIFE: Shen Te! Someone at the door. Where is she anyway?

NEPHEW: She must be getting the breakfast. Mr. Shui Ta will pay for it.

The WIFE *laughs and shuffles to the door. Enter* MR. SHUI TA *and the* CARPENTER.

WIFE: Who is it?

SHUI TA: I am Miss Shen Te's cousin.

WIFE: What?

SHUI TA: My name is Shui Ta.

WIFE: Her cousin?

NEPHEW: Her cousin?

NIECE: But that was a joke. She hasn't got a cousin.

HUSBAND: So early in the morning?

BROTHER: What's all the noise?

SISTER-IN-LAW: This fellow says he's her cousin.

BROTHER: Tell him to prove it.

39

NEPHEW: Right. If you're Shen Te's cousin, prove it by getting the breakfast.

SHUI TA (*whose regime begins as he puts out the lamp to save oil; loudly, to all present, asleep or awake*): Would you all please get dressed! Customers will be coming! I wish to open my shop!

HUSBAND: *Your* shop? Doesn't it belong to our good friend Shen Te?

SHUI TA *shakes his head.*

SISTER-IN-LAW: So we've been cheated. Where *is* the little liar?

SHUI TA: Miss Shen Te has been delayed. She wishes me to tell you there will be nothing she can do—now I am here.

WIFE (*bowled over*): I thought she was good!

NEPHEW: Do you have to believe *him?*

HUSBAND: I don't.

NEPHEW: Then do something.

HUSBAND: Certainly! I'll send out a search party at once. You, you, you, and you, go out and look for Shen Te. (*As the* GRANDFATHER *rises and makes for the door.*) Not you, Grandfather, you and I will hold the fort.

SHUI TA: You won't find Miss Shen Te. She has suspended her hospitable activity for an unlimited period. There are too many of you. She asked me to say: this is a tobacco shop, not a gold mine.

HUSBAND: Shen Te never said a thing like that. Boy, food! There's a bakery on the corner. Stuff your shirt full when they're not looking!

SISTER-IN-LAW: Don't overlook the raspberry tarts.

HUSBAND: And don't let the policeman see you.

The BOY *leaves.*

SHUI TA: Don't you depend on this shop now? Then why give it a bad name by stealing from the bakery?

NEPHEW: Don't listen to him. Let's find Shen Te. She'll give him a piece of her mind.

SISTER-IN-LAW: Don't forget to leave us some breakfast.

BROTHER, SISTER-IN-LAW, *and* NEPHEW *leave.*

SHUI TA (*to the* CARPENTER): You see, Mr. Carpenter, nothing has changed since the poet, eleven hundred years ago, penned these lines:

A governor was asked what was needed
To save the freezing people in the city.
He replied:
"A blanket ten thousand feet long
to cover the city and all its suburbs."

He starts to tidy up the shop.

CARPENTER: Your cousin owes me money. I've got witnesses. For the shelves.

SHUI TA: Yes, I have your bill. (*He takes it out of his pocket.*) Isn't a hundred silver dollars rather a lot?

CARPENTER: No deductions! I have a wife and children.

SHUI TA: How many children?

CARPENTER: Three.

SHUI TA: I'll make you an offer. Twenty silver dollars.

The HUSBAND *laughs.*

CARPENTER: You're crazy. Those shelves are real walnut.

SHUI TA: Very well. Take them away.

CARPENTER: What?

SHUI TA: They cost too much. Please take them away.

WIFE: Not bad! (*And she, too, is laughing.*)

CARPENTER (*a little bewildered*): Call Shen Te, someone! (*To* SHUI TA:) She's *good*!

SHUI TA: Certainly. She's ruined.

CARPENTER (*provoked into taking some of the shelves*): All right, you can keep your tobacco on the floor.

SHUI TA (*to the* HUSBAND): Help him with the shelves.

HUSBAND (*grins and carries one shelf over to the door where the* CARPENTER *now is*): Good-bye, shelves!

CARPENTER (*to the* HUSBAND): You dog! You want my family to starve?

SHUI TA: I repeat my offer. I have no desire to keep my tobacco on the floor. Twenty silver dollars.

CARPENTER (*with desperate aggressiveness*): One hundred!

SHUI TA shows indifference, looks through the window. The HUSBAND picks up several shelves.

CARPENTER (*to HUSBAND*): You needn't smash them against the doorpost, you idiot! (*To SHUI TA:*) These shelves were made to measure. They're no use anywhere else!

SHUI TA: Precisely.

The WIFE squeals with pleasure.

CARPENTER (*giving up, sullenly*): Take the shelves. Pay what you want to pay.

SHUI TA (*smoothly*): Twenty silver dollars.

He places two large coins on the table. The CARPENTER picks them up.

HUSBAND (*brings the shelves back in*): And quite enough too!

CARPENTER (*slinking off*): Quite enough to get drunk on.

HUSBAND (*happily*): Well, we got rid of *him*!

WIFE (*weeping with fun, gives a rendition of the dialogue just spoken*): "Real walnut," says he. "Very well, take them away," says his lordship. "I have three children," says he. "Twenty silver dollars," says his lordship. "They're no use anywhere else," says he. "Pre-cisely," said his lordship! (*She dissolves into shrieks of merriment.*)

SHUI TA: And now: go!

HUSBAND: What's that?

SHUI TA: You're thieves, parasites. I'm giving you this chance. Go!

HUSBAND (*summoning all his ancestral dignity*): That sort deserves no answer. Besides, one should never shout on an empty stomach.

WIFE: Where's that boy?

SHUI TA: Exactly. The boy. I want no stolen goods in this shop. (*Very loudly.*) I strongly advise you to leave! (*But they remain seated, noses in the air. Quietly.*) As you wish. (SHUI TA *goes to the door. A* POLICE-MAN *appears.* SHUI TA *bows.*) I am addressing the officer in charge of this precinct?

POLICEMAN: That's right, Mr., um, what was the name, sir?

SHUI TA: Mr. Shui Ta.

POLICEMAN: Yes, of course, sir.

They exchange a smile.

SHUI TA: Nice weather we're having.

POLICEMAN: A little on the warm side, sir.

SHUI TA: Oh, a little on the warm side.

HUSBAND (*whispering to the* WIFE): If he keeps it up till the boy's back, we're done for. (*Tries to signal* SHUI TA.)

SHUI TA (*ignoring the signal*): Weather, of course, is one thing indoors, another out on the dusty street!

POLICEMAN: Oh, quite another, sir!

WIFE (*to the* HUSBAND): It's all right as long as he's standing in the doorway—the boy will see him.

SHUI TA: Step inside for a moment! It's quite cool indoors. My cousin and I have just opened the place. And we attach the greatest importance to being on good terms with the, um, authorities.

POLICEMAN (*entering*): Thank you, Mr. Shui Ta. It *is* cool!

HUSBAND (*whispering to the* WIFE): And now the boy *won't* see him.

SHUI TA (*showing* HUSBAND *and* WIFE *to the* POLICEMAN): Visitors, I think my cousin knows them. They were just leaving.

HUSBAND (*defeated*): Ye-e-es, we were . . . just leaving.

SHUI TA: I'll tell my cousin you couldn't wait.

Noise from the street. Shouts of "Stop, Thief!"

POLICEMAN: What's that?

The BOY *is in the doorway with cakes and buns and rolls spilling out of his shirt. The* WIFE *signals desperately to him to leave. He gets the idea.*

POLICEMAN: No, you don't! (*He grabs the* BOY *by the collar.*) Where's all this from?

BOY (*vaguely pointing*): Down the street.

POLICEMAN (*grimly*): So that's it. (*Prepares to arrest the* BOY.)

WIFE (*stepping in*): And *we* knew nothing about it. (*To the* BOY:) Nasty little thief!

POLICEMAN (*dryly*): Can you clarify the situation, Mr. Shui Ta?

SHUI TA *is silent.*

POLICEMAN (*who understands silence*): Aha. You're all coming with me—to the station.

SHUI TA: I can hardly say how sorry I am that my establishment . . .

WIFE: Oh, he saw the boy leave not ten minutes ago!

SHUI TA: And to conceal the theft asked a policeman in?

POLICEMAN: Don't listen to her, Mr. Shui Ta, I'll be happy to relieve you of their presence one and all! (*To all three:*) Out! (*He drives them before him.*)

GRANDFATHER (*leaving last, gravely*): Good morning!

POLICEMAN: Good morning!

SHUI TA, *left alone, continues to tidy up.* MRS. MI TZU *breezes in.*

MRS. MI TZU: You're her cousin, are you? Then have the goodness to explain what all this means—police dragging people from a respectable house! By what right does your Miss Shen Te turn my property into a house of assignation?—Well, as you see, I know all!

SHUI TA: Yes. My cousin has the worst possible reputation: that of being poor.

MRS. MI TZU: No sentimental rubbish, Mr. Shui Ta. Your cousin was a common . . .

SHUI TA: Pauper. Let's use the uglier word.

MRS. MI TZU: I'm speaking of her conduct, not her earnings. But there must have *been* earnings, or how did she buy all this? Several elderly gentlemen took care of it, I suppose. I repeat: this is a respectable house! I have tenants who prefer not to live under the same roof with such a person.

SHUI TA (*quietly*): How much do you want?

MRS. MI TZU (*he is ahead of her now*): I beg your pardon.

SHUI TA: To reassure yourself. To reassure your tenants. How much will it cost?

MRS. MI TZU: You're a cool customer.

SHUI TA (*picking up the lease*): The rent is high. (*He reads on.*) I assume it's payable by the month?

MRS. MI TZU: Not in her case.

SHUI TA (*looking up*): What?

MRS. MI TZU: Six months' rent payable in advance. Two hundred silver dollars.

SHUI TA: Six . . . ! Sheer usury! And where am I to find it?

MRS. MI TZU: You should have thought of that before.

SHUI TA: Have you no heart, Mrs. Mi Tzu? It's true Shen Te acted foolishly, being kind to all those people, but she'll improve with time. I'll see to it she does. She'll work her fingers to the bone to pay her rent, and all the time be as quiet as a mouse, as humble as a fly.

MRS. MI TZU: Her social background . . .

SHUI TA: Out of the depths! She came out of the depths! And before she'll go back there, she'll work, sacrifice, shrink from nothing. . . . Such a tenant is worth her weight in gold, Mrs. Mi Tzu.

MRS. MI TZU: It's silver we were talking about, Mr. Shui Ta. Two hundred silver dollars or . . .

Enter the POLICEMAN.

POLICEMAN: Am I intruding, Mr. Shui Ta?

MRS. MI TZU: This tobacco shop is well known to the police, I see.

POLICEMAN: Mr. Shui Ta has done us a service, Mrs. Mi Tzu. I am here to present our official felicitations!

MRS. MI TZU: That means less than nothing to me, sir. Mr. Shui Ta, all I can say is: I hope your cousin will find my terms acceptable. Good day, gentlemen. (*Exit.*)

SHUI TA: Good day, ma'am.

Pause.

POLICEMAN: Mrs. Mi Tzu a bit of a stumbling block, sir?

SHUI TA: She wants six months' rent in advance.

POLICEMAN: And you haven't got it, eh? (SHUI TA *is silent*.) But surely you can get it, sir? A man like you?

SHUI TA: What about a woman like Shen Te?

POLICEMAN: You're not staying, sir?

SHUI TA: No, and I won't be back. Do you smoke?

POLICEMAN (*taking two cigars, and placing them both in his pocket*): Thank you, sir—I see your point. Miss Te—let's mince no words—Miss Shen Te lived by selling herself. "What else could she have done?" you ask. "How else was she to pay the rent?" True. But the fact remains, Mr. Shui Ta, it is not respectable. Why not? A very deep question. But, in the first place, love—love isn't bought and sold like cigars, Mr. Shui Ta. In the second place, it isn't respectable to go waltzing off with someone that's paying his way, so to speak—it must be for love! Thirdly and lastly, as the proverb has it: not for a handful of rice but for love! (*Pause. He is thinking hard.*) "Well," you may say, "and what good is all this wisdom if the milk's already spilt?" Miss Shen Te is what she is. Is *where* she is. We have to face the fact that if she doesn't get hold of six months' rent pronto, she'll be back on the streets. The question then as I see it— everything in this world is a matter of opinion—the question as I see it is: *how* is she to get hold of this rent? How? Mr. Shui Ta: I don't know. (*Pause.*) I take that back, sir. It's just come to me. A husband. We must find her a husband!

Enter a little OLD WOMAN.

OLD WOMAN: A good cheap cigar for my husband, we'll have been married forty years tomorrow and we're having a little celebration.

SHUI TA: Forty years? And you still want to celebrate?

OLD WOMAN: As much as we can afford to. We have the carpet shop across the square. We'll be good neighbors, I hope?

SHUI TA: I hope so too.

POLICEMAN (*who keeps making discoveries*): Mr. Shui Ta, you know what we need? We need capital. And how do we acquire capital? We get married.

SHUI TA (*to* OLD WOMAN): I'm afraid I've been pestering this gentleman with my personal worries.

POLICEMAN (*lyrically*): We can't pay six months' rent, so what do we do? We marry money.

SHUI TA: That might not be easy.

POLICEMAN: Oh, I don't know. She's a good match. Has a nice, growing business. (*To the* OLD WOMAN:) What do you think?

OLD WOMAN (*undecided*): Well—

POLICEMAN: Should she put an ad in the paper?

OLD WOMAN (*not eager to commit herself*): Well, if *she* agrees—

POLICEMAN: I'll write it for her. *You* lend us a hand, and *we* write an ad for you! (*He chuckles away to him-*

self, takes out his notebook, wets the stump of a pencil between his lips, and writes away.)

SHUI TA (*slowly*): Not a bad idea.

POLICEMAN: "What . . . *respectable* . . . man . . . with small capital . . . widower . . . not excluded . . . desires . . . marriage . . . into flourishing . . . tobacco shop?" And now let's add: "Am . . . pretty . . ." No! . . . "Prepossessing appearance."

SHUI TA: If you don't think that's an exaggeration?

OLD WOMAN: Oh, not a bit. I've seen her.

The POLICEMAN *tears the page out of his notebook, and hands it over to* SHUI TA.

SHUI TA (*with horror in his voice*): How much luck we need to keep our heads above water! How many ideas! How many friends! (*To the* POLICEMAN:) Thank you, sir, I think I see my way clear.

3

Evening in the municipal park. Noise of a plane overhead.
YANG SUN, *a young man in rags, is following the plane*
with his eyes: one can tell that the machine is describing
a curve above the park. YANG SUN *then takes a rope out*
of his pocket, looking anxiously about him as he does so.
He moves toward a large willow. Enter two prostitutes, one
the OLD WHORE, *the other the* NIECE *whom we have al-*
ready met.

NIECE: Hello. Coming with me?

YANG SUN (*taken aback*): If you'd like to buy me a dinner.

OLD WHORE: Buy you a dinner! (*To the* NIECE:) Oh, we
    know him—it's the unemployed pilot. Waste no time
    on him!

NIECE: But he's the only man left in the park. And it's
    going to rain.

OLD WHORE: Oh, how do you know?

> *And they pass by.* YANG SUN *again looks about him,*
> *again takes his rope, and this time throws it round a*
> *branch of the willow tree. Again he is interrupted. It*
> *is the two prostitutes returning—and in such a hurry*
> *they don't notice him.*

NIECE: It's going to pour!

> *Enter* SHEN TE.

OLD WHORE: There's that *gorgon* Shen Te! That *drove* your family out into the cold!

NIECE: It wasn't her. It was that cousin of hers. She offered to pay for the cakes. I've nothing against her.

OLD WHORE: I have, though. (*So that* SHEN TE *can hear.*) Now where could the little lady be off to? She may be rich now but that won't stop her snatching our young men, will it?

SHEN TE: I'm going to the tearoom by the pond.

NIECE: Is it true what they say? You're marrying a widower —with three children?

SHEN TE: Yes. I'm just going to see him.

YANG SUN (*his patience at breaking point*): Move on there! This is a park, not a whorehouse!

OLD WHORE: Shut your mouth!

But the two prostitutes leave.

YANG SUN: Even in the farthest corner of the park, even when it's raining, you can't get rid of them! (*He spits.*)

SHEN TE (*overhearing this*): And what right have you to scold them? (*But at this point she sees the rope.*) Oh!

YANG SUN: Well, what are you staring at?

SHEN TE: That rope. What is it for?

YANG SUN: Think! Think! I haven't a penny. Even if I

had, I wouldn't spend it on you. I'd buy a drink of
water.

The rain starts.

SHEN TE (*still looking at the rope*): What is the rope for?
You mustn't!

YANG SUN: What's it to you? Clear out!

SHEN TE (*irrelevantly*): It's raining.

YANG SUN: Well, don't try to come under this tree.

SHEN TE: Oh, no. (*She stays in the rain.*)

YANG SUN: Now go away. (*Pause.*) For one thing, I don't
like your looks, you're bowlegged.

SHEN TE (*indignantly*): That's not true!

YANG SUN: Well, don't show 'em to me. Look, it's raining.
You better come under this tree.

Slowly, she takes shelter under the tree.

SHEN TE: Why did you want to do it?

YANG SUN: You really want to know? (*Pause.*) To get rid
of you! (*Pause.*) You know what a flyer is?

SHEN TE: Oh yes, I've met a lot of pilots. At the tearoom.

YANG SUN: You call *them* flyers? Think they know what
a machine is? Just 'cause they have leather helmets?
They gave the airfield director a bribe, that's the
way *those* fellows got up in the air! Try one of them

out sometime. "Go up to two thousand feet," tell them, "then let it fall, then pick it up again with a flick of the wrist at the last moment." Know what he'll say to that? "It's not in my contract." Then again, there's the landing problem. It's like landing on your own backside. It's no different, planes are human. Those fools don't understand. (*Pause.*) And I'm the biggest fool for reading the book on flying in the Peking school and skipping the page where it says: "We've got enough flyers and we don't need you." I'm a mail pilot with no mail. You understand that?

SHEN TE (*shyly*): Yes. I do.

YANG SUN: No, you don't. You'd never understand that.

SHEN TE: When we were little we had a crane with a broken wing. He made friends with us and was very good-natured about our jokes. He would strut along behind us and call out to stop us going too fast for him. But every spring and autumn when the cranes flew over the villages in great swarms, he got quite restless. (*Pause.*) I understand that. (*She bursts out crying.*)

YANG SUN: Don't!

SHEN TE (*quieting down*): No.

YANG SUN: It's bad for the complexion.

SHEN TE (*sniffing*): I've stopped.

She dries her tears on her big sleeve. Leaning against the tree, but not looking at her, he reaches for her face.

YANG SUN: You can't even wipe your own face. (*He is wiping it for her with his handkerchief. Pause.*)

SHEN TE (*still sobbing*): I don't know *anything!*

YANG SUN: You interrupted me! What for?

SHEN TE: It's such a rainy day. You only wanted to do . . . *that* because it's such a rainy day. (*To the audience*:)

In our country
The evenings should never be somber
High bridges over rivers
The gray hour between night and morning
And the long, long winter:
Such things are dangerous
For, with all the misery,
A very little is enough
And men throw away an unbearable life.

Pause.

YANG SUN: Talk about yourself for a change.

SHEN TE: What about me? I have a shop.

YANG SUN (*incredulous*): You have a shop, have you? Never thought of walking the streets?

SHEN TE: I did walk the streets. Now I have a shop.

YANG SUN (*ironically*): A gift of the gods, I suppose!

SHEN TE: How did you know?

YANG SUN (*even more ironical*): One fine evening the gods turned up saying: here's some money!

SHEN TE (*quickly*): One fine morning.

YANG SUN (*fed up*): This isn't much of an entertainment.

Pause.

SHEN TE: I can play the zither a little. (*Pause.*) And I can
mimic men. (*Pause.*) I got the shop, so the first
thing I did was to give my zither away. I can be as
stupid as a fish now, I said to myself, and it won't
matter.

I'm rich now, I said
I walk alone, I sleep alone
For a whole year, I said
I'll have nothing to do with a man.

YANG SUN: And now you're marrying one! The one at
the tearoom by the pond?

SHEN TE *is silent.*

YANG SUN: What do you know about love?

SHEN TE: Everything.

YANG SUN: Nothing. (*Pause.*) Or d'you just mean you
enjoyed it?

SHEN TE: No.

YANG SUN (*again without turning to look at her, he strokes
her cheek with his hand*): You like that?

SHEN TE: Yes.

YANG SUN (*breaking off*): You're easily satisfied, I must
say. (*Pause.*) What a town!

SHEN TE: You have no friends?

YANG SUN (*defensively*): Yes, I have! (*Change of tone.*)
But they don't want to hear I'm still unemployed.
"What?" they ask. "Is there still water in the sea?"
You have friends?

SHEN TE (*hesitating*): Just a . . . cousin.

YANG SUN: Watch him carefully.

SHEN TE: He only came once. Then he went away. He
won't be back. (YANG SUN *is looking away.*) But to
be without hope, they say, is to be without goodness!

Pause.

YANG SUN: Go on talking. A voice is a voice.

SHEN TE: Once, when I was a little girl, I fell, with a load
of brushwood. An old man picked me up. He gave
me a penny too. Isn't it funny how people who don't
have very much like to give some of it away? They
must like to show what they can do, and how could
they show it better than by being kind? Being wicked
is just like being clumsy. When we sing a song, or
build a machine, or plant some rice, we're being
kind. You're kind.

YANG SUN: You make it sound easy.

SHEN TE: Oh, no. (*Little pause.*) Oh! A drop of rain!

YANG SUN: Where'd you feel it?

SHEN TE: Between the eyes.

YANG SUN: Near the right eye? Or the left?

SHEN TE: Near the left eye.

YANG SUN: Oh, good. (*He is getting sleepy.*) So you're through with men, eh?

SHEN TE (*with a smile*): But I'm not bowlegged.

YANG SUN: Perhaps not.

SHEN TE: Definitely not.

Pause.

YANG SUN (*leaning wearily against the willow*): I haven't had a drop to drink all day, I haven't eaten anything for *two* days. I couldn't love you if I tried.

Pause.

SHEN TE: I like it in the rain.

Enter WONG *the water seller, singing.*

THE SONG OF THE WATER SELLER IN THE RAIN

"Buy my water," I am yelling
And my fury restraining
For no water I'm selling
'Cause it's raining, 'cause it's raining!
I keep yelling: "Buy my water!"
But no one's buying
Athirst and dying
And drinking and paying!
Buy water!
Buy water, you dogs!

Nice to dream of lovely weather!
Thnk of all the consternation
Were there no precipitation

Half a dozen years together!
> Can't you hear them shrieking: "Water!"
> Pretending they adore me?
> They all would go down on their knees
>> before me!
> Down on your knees!
> Go down on your knees, you dogs!

What are lawns and hedges thinking?
What are fields and forests saying?
"At the clouds's breast we are drinking!
And we've no idea who's paying!"
> I keep yelling: "Buy my water!"
> But no one's buying
> Athirst and dying
> And drinking and paying!
> Buy water!
> Buy water, you dogs!

The rain has stopped now. SHEN TE *sees* WONG *and
runs toward him.*

SHEN TE: Wong! You're back! Your carrying pole's at the
shop.

WONG: Oh, thank you, Shen Te. And how is life treating
you?

SHEN TE: I've just met a brave and clever man. And I
want to buy him a cup of your water.

WONG (*bitterly*): Throw back your head and open your
mouth and you'll have all the water you need—

SHEN TE (*tenderly*):

> I want *your* water, Wong
> The water that has tired you so

The water that you carried all this way
The water that is hard to sell because
    it's been raining.

I need it for the young man over there—he's a flyer!

A flyer is a bold man:
Braving the storms
In company with the clouds
He crosses the heavens
And brings to friends in faraway lands
The friendly mail!

She pays WONG, *and runs over to* YANG SUN *with the cup. But* YANG SUN *is fast asleep.*

SHEN TE (*calling to* WONG, *with a laugh*): He's fallen asleep! Despair and rain and I have worn him out!

3a

Wong's den. The sewer pipe is transparent, and the GODS *again appear to* WONG *in a dream.*

WONG (*radiant*): I've seen her, illustrious ones! And she hasn't changed!

FIRST GOD: That's good to hear.

WONG: She loves someone.

FIRST GOD: Let's hope the experience gives her the strength to stay good!

WONG: It does. She's doing good deeds all the time.

FIRST GOD: Ah? What sort? What sort of good deeds, Wong?

WONG: Well, she has a kind word for everybody.

FIRST GOD (*eagerly*): And then?

WONG: Hardly anyone leaves her shop without tobacco in his pocket—even if he can't pay for it.

FIRST GOD: Not bad at all. Next?

WONG: She's putting up a family of eight.

FIRST GOD (*gleefully, to the* SECOND GOD): Eight! (*To* WONG:) And that's not all, of course!

WONG: She bought a cup of water from me even though it was raining.

FIRST GOD: Yes, yes, yes, all these smaller good deeds!

WONG: Even they run into money. A little tobacco shop doesn't make so much.

FIRST GOD (*sententiously*): A prudent gardener works miracles on the smallest plot.

WONG: She hands out rice every morning. That eats up half her earnings.

FIRST GOD (*a little disappointed*): Well, as a beginning . . .

WONG: They call her the Angel of the Slums—whatever the carpenter may say!

FIRST GOD: What's this? A carpenter speaks ill of her?

WONG: Oh, he only says her shelves weren't paid for in full.

SECOND GOD (*who has a bad cold and can't pronounce his n's and m's*): What's this? Not paying a carpenter? Why was that?

WONG: I suppose she didn't have the money.

SECOND GOD (*severely*): One pays what one owes, that's in our book of rules! First the letter of the law, then the spirit.

WONG: But it wasn't Shen Te, illustrious ones, it was her cousin. She called *him* in to help.

SECOND GOD: Then her cousin must never darken her threshold again!

WONG: Very well, illustrious ones! But in fairness to Shen Te, let me say that her cousin is a businessman.

FIRST GOD: Perhaps we should inquire what is customary? I find business quite unintelligible. But everybody's doing it. Business! Did the Seven Good Kings do business? Did Kung the Just sell fish?

SECOND GOD: In any case, such a thing must not occur again!

The GODS start to leave.

THIRD GOD: Forgive us for taking this tone with you, Wong, we haven't been getting enough sleep. The rich recommend us to the poor, and the poor tell us they haven't enough room.

SECOND GOD: Feeble, feeble, the best of them!

FIRST GOD: No great deeds! No heroic daring!

THIRD GOD: On such a *small* scale!

SECOND GOD: Sincere, yes, but what is actually *achieved?*

One can no longer hear them.

WONG (*calling after them*): I've thought of something, illustrious ones: Perhaps you shouldn't ask—too—much—all—at—once!

4

The square in front of Shen Te's tobacco shop. Besides Shen Te's place, two other shops are seen: the carpet shop and a barber's. Morning. Outside Shen Te's the GRAND-FATHER, *the* SISTER-IN-LAW, *the* UNEMPLOYED MAN, *and* MRS. SHIN *stand waiting.*

SISTER-IN-LAW: She's been out all night again.

MRS. SHIN: No sooner did we get rid of that crazy cousin of hers than Shen Te herself starts carrying on! Maybe she does give us an ounce of rice now and then, but can you depend on her? Can you depend on her?

Loud voices from the barber's.

VOICE OF SHU FU: What are you doing in my shop? Get out—at once!

VOICE OF WONG: But sir. They all let me sell . . .

WONG *comes staggering out of the barber's shop pursued by* MR. SHU FU, *the barber, a fat man carrying a heavy curling iron.*

SHU FU: Get out, I said! Pestering my customers with your slimy old water! Get out! Take your cup!

He holds out the cup. WONG *reaches out for it.* MR. SHU FU *strikes his hand with the curling iron, which is hot.* WONG *howls.*

SHU FU: You had it coming, my man!

Puffing, he returns to his shop. The UNEMPLOYED
MAN *picks up the cup and gives it to* WONG.

UNEMPLOYED MAN: You can report that to the police.

WONG: My hand! It's smashed up!

UNEMPLOYED MAN: Any bones broken?

WONG: I can't move my fingers.

UNEMPLOYED MAN: Sit down. I'll put some water on it.

WONG *sits.*

MRS. SHIN: The water won't cost you anything.

SISTER-IN-LAW: You might have got a bandage from Miss
Shen Te till she took to staying out all night. It's a
scandal.

MRS. SHIN (*despondently*): If you ask me, she's forgotten
we ever existed!

Enter SHEN TE *down the street, with a dish of rice.*

SHEN TE (*to the audience*): How wonderful to see Setzuan
in the early morning! I always used to stay in bed
with my dirty blanket over my head afraid to wake
up. This morning I saw the newspapers being delivered by little boys, the streets being washed by
strong men, and fresh vegetables coming in from the
country on ox carts. It's a long walk from where Yang
Sun lives, but I feel lighter at every step. They say
you walk on air when you're in love, but it's even
better walking on the rough earth, on the hard
cement. In the early morning, the old city looks like

a great heap of rubbish! Nice, though, with all its
little lights. And the sky, so pink, so transparent,
before the dust comes and muddies it! What a lot
you miss if you never see your city rising from its
slumbers like an honest old craftsman pumping his
lungs full of air and reaching for his tools, as the poet
says! (*Cheerfully, to her waiting guests:*) Good morning, everyone, here's your rice! (*Distributing the rice,
she comes upon* WONG.) Good morning, Wong, I'm
quite lightheaded today. On my way over, I looked at
myself in all the shop windows. I'd love to be beautiful.

She slips into the carpet shop. MR. SHU FU *has just
emerged from his shop.*

SHU FU (*to the audience*): It surprises me how beautiful
Miss Shen Te is looking today! I never gave her a
passing thought before. But now I've been gazing
upon her comely form for exactly three minutes! I
begin to suspect I am in love with her. She is over-
poweringly attractive! (*Crossly, to* WONG:) Be off
with you, rascal!

He returns to his shop. SHEN TE *comes back out of
the carpet shop with the* OLD MAN, *its proprietor, and
his wife—whom we have already met—the* OLD
WOMAN. SHEN TE *is wearing a shawl. The* OLD MAN
is holding up a looking glass for her.

OLD WOMAN: Isn't it lovely? We'll give you a reduction because there's a little hole in it.

SHEN TE (*looking at another shawl on the* OLD WOMAN'S
arm): The other one's nice too.

OLD WOMAN (*smiling*): Too bad there's no hole in that!

SHEN TE: That's right. My shop doesn't make very much.

OLD WOMAN: And your good deeds eat it all up! Be more careful, my dear. . . .

SHEN TE (*trying on the shawl with the hole*): Just now, I'm lightheaded! Does the color suit me?

OLD WOMAN: You'd better ask a man.

SHEN TE (*to the* OLD MAN): Does the color suit me?

OLD MAN: You'd better ask your young friend.

SHEN TE: I'd like to have your opinion.

OLD MAN: It suits you very well. But wear it this way: the dull side out.

SHEN TE *pays up.*

OLD WOMAN: If you decide you don't like it, you can exchange it. (*She pulls* SHEN TE *to one side.*) Has he got money?

SHEN TE (*with a laugh*): Yang Sun? Oh, no.

OLD WOMAN: Then how're you going to pay your rent?

SHEN TE: I'd forgotten about that.

OLD WOMAN: And next Monday is the first of the month! Miss Shen Te, I've got something to say to you. After we (*indicating her husband*) got to know you, we had our doubts about that marriage ad. We thought it would be better if you'd let *us* help you. Out of our savings. We reckon we could lend you two hundred silver dollars. We don't need anything in writing—you could pledge us your tobacco stock.

SHEN TE: You're prepared to lend money to a person like me?

OLD WOMAN: It's folks like you that need it. We'd think twice about lending anything to your cousin.

OLD MAN (*coming up*): All settled, my dear?

SHEN TE: I wish the gods could have heard what your wife was just saying, Mr. Ma. They're looking for good people who're happy—and helping me makes you happy because you know it was love that got me into difficulties!

The OLD COUPLE *smile knowingly at each other.*

OLD MAN: And here's the money, Miss Shen Te.

He hands her an envelope. SHEN TE *takes it. She bows. They bow back. They return to their shop.*

SHEN TE (*holding up her envelope*): Look, Wong, here's six months' rent! Don't you believe in miracles now? And how do you like my new shawl?

WONG: For the young fellow I saw you with in the park?

SHEN TE *nods.*

MRS. SHIN: Never mind all that. It's time you took a look at his hand!

SHEN TE: Have you hurt your hand?

MRS. SHIN: That barber smashed it with his hot curling iron. Right in front of our eyes.

SHEN TE (*shocked at herself*): And I never noticed! We must get you to a doctor this minute or who knows what will happen?

UNEMPLOYED MAN: It's not a doctor he should see, it's a judge. He can ask for compensation. The barber's filthy rich.

WONG: You think I have a chance?

MRS. SHIN (*with relish*): If it's really good and smashed. But is it?

WONG: I think so. It's very swollen. Could I get a pension?

MRS. SHIN: You'd need a witness.

WONG: Well, you all saw it. You could all testify.

He looks round. The UNEMPLOYED MAN, *the* GRAND-FATHER, *and the* SISTER-IN-LAW *are all sitting against the wall of the shop eating rice. Their concentration on eating is complete.*

SHEN TE (*to* MRS. SHIN): You saw it yourself.

MRS. SHIN: I want nothing to do with the police. It's against my principles.

SHEN TE (*to* SISTER-IN-LAW): What about you?

SISTER-IN-LAW: Me? I wasn't looking.

SHEN TE (*to the* GRANDFATHER, *coaxingly*): Grandfather, *you'll* testify, won't you?

SISTER-IN-LAW: And a lot of good that will do. He's simple-minded.

SHEN TE (*to the* UNEMPLOYED MAN): You seem to be the only witness left.

UNEMPLOYED MAN: My testimony would only hurt him. I've been picked up twice for begging.

SHEN TE:
Your brother is assaulted, and you shut your eyes?
He is hit, cries out in pain, and you are silent?
The beast prowls, chooses and seizes his victim, and
    you say:
"Because we showed no displeasure, he has spared
    us."

If no one present will be a witness, I will. I'll say
I saw it.

MRS. SHIN (*solemnly*): The name for that is perjury.

WONG: I don't know if I can accept that. Though maybe I'll have to. (*Looking at his hand.*) Is it swollen enough, do you think? The swelling's not going down?

UNEMPLOYED MAN: No, no. the swelling's holding up well.

WONG: Yes. It's *more* swollen if anything. Maybe my wrist is broken after all. I'd better see a judge at once.

Holding his hand very carefully, and fixing his eyes on it, he runs off. MRS. SHIN *goes quickly into the barber's shop.*

UNEMPLOYED MAN (*seeing her*): She is getting on the right side of Mr. Shu Fu.

In front of the inner curtain. Enter SHEN TE, *carrying Shui Ta's mask. She sings.*

THE SONG OF DEFENSELESSNESS

In our country
A useful man needs luck
Only if he finds strong backers
Can he prove himself useful.
The good can't defend themselves and
Even the gods are defenseless.

Oh, why don't the gods have their own ammunition
And launch against badness their own expedition
Enthroning the good and preventing sedition
And bringing the world to a peaceful condition?

Oh, why don't the gods do the buying and selling
Injustice forbidding, starvation dispelling
Give bread to each city and joy to each dwelling?
Oh, why don't the gods do the buying and selling?

She puts on SHUI TA's *mask and sings in his voice.*

You can only help one of your luckless brothers
By trampling down a dozen others.

Why is it the gods do not feel indignation
And come down in fury to end exploitation
Defeat all defeat and forbid desperation
Refusing to tolerate such toleration?

Why is it?

5

Shen Te's tobacco shop. Behind the counter, MR. SHUI TA, *reading the paper.* MRS. SHIN *is cleaning up. She talks and he takes no notice.*

MRS. SHIN: And when certain rumors get about, what *happens* to a little place like this? It goes to pot. *I* know. So, if you want my advice, Mr. Shui Ta, find out just what has been going on between Miss Shen Te and that Yang Sun from Yellow Street. And remember: a certain interest in Miss Shen Te has been expressed by the barber next door, a man with twelve houses and only one wife, who, for that matter, is likely to drop off at any time. A certain interest has been expressed. He was even inquiring about her means and, if *that* doesn't prove a man is getting serious, what would? (*Still getting no response, she leaves with her bucket.*)

YANG SUN'S VOICE: Is that Miss Shen Te's tobacco shop?

MRS. SHIN'S VOICE: Yes, it is, but it's Mr. Shui Ta who's here today.

SHUI TA runs to the mirror with the short, light steps of SHEN TE, and is just about to start primping, when he realizes his mistake, and turns away, with a short laugh. Enter YANG SUN. MRS. SHIN enters behind him and slips into the back room to eavesdrop.

YANG SUN: I am Yang Sun. (SHUI TA *bows.*) Is Shen Te in?

SHUI TA: No.

YANG SUN: I guess you know our relationship? (*He is inspecting the stock.*) Quite a place! And I thought she was just talking big. I'll be flying again, all right. (*He takes a cigar, solicits and receives a light from* SHUI TA.) You think we can squeeze the other three hundred out of the tobacco stock?

SHUI TA: May I ask if it is your intention to sell at once?

YANG SUN: It was decent of her to come out with the two hundred but they aren't much use with the other three hundred still missing.

SHUI TA: Shen Te was overhasty promising so much. She might have to sell the shop itself to raise it. Haste, they say, is the wind that blows the house down.

YANG SUN: Oh, she isn't a girl to keep a man waiting. For one thing or the other, if you take my meaning.

SHUI TA: I take your meaning.

YANG SUN (*leering*): Uh, huh.

SHUI TA: Would you explain what the five hundred silver dollars are for?

YANG SUN: Want to sound me out? Very well. The director of the Peking airfield is a friend of mine from flying school. I give him five hundred: he gets me the job.

SHUI TA: The price is high.

YANG SUN: Not as these things go. He'll have to fire

one of the present pilots—for negligence. Only the man he has in mind isn't negligent. Not easy, you understand. You needn't mention that part of it to Shen Te.

SHUI TA (*looking intently at* YANG SUN): Mr. Yang Sun, you are asking my cousin to give up her possessions, leave her friends, and place her entire fate in your hands. I presume you intend to marry her?

YANG SUN: I'd be prepared to.

Slight pause.

SHUI TA: Those two hundred silver dollars would pay the rent here for six months. If you were Shen Te wouldn't you be tempted to continue in business?

YANG SUN: What? Can you imagine Yang Sun the flyer behind a counter? (*In an oily voice.*) "A strong cigar or a mild one, worthy sir?" Not in this century!

SHUI TA: My cousin wishes to follow the promptings of her heart, and, from her own point of view, she may even have what is called the right to love. Accordingly, she has commissioned me to help you to this post. There is nothing here that I am not empowered to turn immediately into cash. Mrs. Mi Tzu, the landlady, will advise me about the sale.

Enter MRS. MI TZU.

MRS. MI TZU: Good morning, Mr. Shui Ta, you wish to see me about the rent? As you know it falls due the day after tomorrow.

SHUI TA: Circumstances have changed, Mrs. Mi Tzu: my

cousin is getting married. Her future husband here, Mr. Yang Sun, will be taking her to Peking. I am interested in selling the tobacco stock.

MRS. MI TZU: How much are you asking, Mr. Shui Ta?

YANG SUN: Three hundred sil—

SHUI TA: Five hundred silver dollars.

MRS. MI TZU: How much did she pay for it, Mr. Shui Ta?

SHUI TA: A thousand. And very little has been sold.

MRS. MI TZU: She was robbed. But I'll make you a special offer if you'll promise to be out by the day after tomorrow. Three hundred silver dollars.

YANG SUN (*shrugging*): Take it, man, take it.

SHUI TA: It is not enough.

YANG SUN: Why not? Why not? Certainly, it's enough.

SHUI TA: Five hundred silver dollars.

YANG SUN: But why? We only need three!

SHUI TA (*to* MRS. MI TZU): Excuse me. (*Takes* YANG SUN *on one side.*) The tobacco stock is pledged to the old couple who gave my cousin the two hundred.

YANG SUN: Is it in writing?

SHUI TA: No.

YANG SUN (*to* MRS. MI TZU): Three hundred will do.

MRS. MI TZU: Of course, I need an assurance that Miss Shen Te is not in debt.

YANG SUN: Mr. Shui Ta?

SHUI TA: She is not in debt.

YANG SUN: When can you let us have the money?

MRS. MI TZU: The day after tomorrow. And remember: I'm doing this because I have a soft spot in my heart for young lovers! (*Exit.*)

YANG SUN (*calling after her*): Boxes, jars and sacks—three hundred for the lot and the pain's over! (*To* SHUI TA:) Where else can we raise money by the day after tomorrow?

SHUI TA: Nowhere. Haven't you enough for the trip and the first few weeks?

YANG SUN: Oh, certainly.

SHUI TA: How much, exactly.

YANG SUN: Oh, I'll dig it up, even if I have to steal it.

SHUI TA: I see.

YANG SUN: Well, don't fall off the roof. I'll get to Peking somehow.

SHUI TA: Two people can't travel for nothing.

YANG SUN (*not giving* SHUI TA *a chance to answer*): I'm leaving *her* behind. No millstones round *my* neck!

SHUI TA: Oh.

YANG SUN: Don't look at me like that!

SHUI TA: How precisely is my cousin to live?

YANG SUN: Oh, you'll think of something.

SHUI TA: A small request, Mr. Yang Sun. Leave the two hundred silver dollars here until you can show me two tickets for Peking.

YANG SUN: You learn to mind your own business, Mr. Shui Ta.

SHUI TA: I'm afraid Miss Shen Te may not wish to sell the shop when she discovers that . . .

YANG SUN: You don't know women. She'll want to. Even then.

SHUI TA (*a slight outburst*): She is a human being, sir! And not devoid of common sense!

YANG SUN: Shen Te is a woman: she *is* devoid of common sense. I only have to lay my hand on her shoulder, and church bells ring.

SHUI TA (*with difficulty*): Mr. Yang Sun!

YANG SUN: Mr. Shui Whatever-it-is!

SHUI TA: My cousin is devoted to you . . . because . . .

YANG SUN: Because I have my hands on her breasts. Give me a cigar. (*He takes one for himself, stuffs a few more in his pocket, then changes his mind and takes the whole box.*) Tell her I'll marry her, then bring me the three hundred. Or let her bring it. One or the other. (*Exit.*)

MRS. SHIN (*sticking her head out of the back room*): Well, he has your cousin under his thumb, and doesn't care if all Yellow Street knows it!

SHUI TA (*crying out*): I've lost my shop! And he doesn't love me! (*He runs berserk through the room, repeating these lines incoherently. Then stops suddenly, and addresses* MRS. SHIN.) Mrs. Shin, you grew up in the gutter, like me. Are we lacking in hardness? I doubt it. If you steal a penny from me, I'll take you by the throat till you spit it out! You'd do the same to me. The times are bad, this city is hell, but we're like ants, we keep coming, up and up the walls, however smooth! Till bad luck comes. Being in love, for instance. One weakness is enough, and love is the deadliest.

MRS. SHIN (*emerging from the back room*): You should have a little talk with Mr. Shu Fu, the barber. He's a real gentleman and just the thing for your cousin. (*She runs off.*)

SHUI TA:

A caress becomes a stranglehold
A sigh of love turns to a cry of fear
Why are there vultures circling in the air?
A girl is going to meet her lover.

SHUI TA *sits down and* MR. SHU FU *enters with* MRS. SHIN.

SHUI TA: Mr. Shu Fu?

SHU FU: Mr. Shui Ta.

They both bow.

SHUI TA: I am told that you have expressed a certain interest in my cousin Shen Te. Let me set aside all propriety and confess: she is at this moment in grave
danger.

SHU FU: Oh, dear!

SHUI TA: She has lost her shop, Mr. Shu Fu.

SHU FU: The charm of Miss Shen Te, Mr. Shui Ta, derives
from the goodness, not of her shop, but of her heart.
Men call her the Angel of the Slums.

SHUI TA: Yet her goodness has cost her two hundred
silver dollars in a single day: we must put a stop to it.

SHU FU: Permit me to differ, Mr. Shui Ta. Let us, rather,
open wide the gates to such goodness! Every morning,
with pleasure tinged by affection, I watch her charita-
ble ministrations. For they are hungry, and she giveth
them to eat! Four of them, to be precise. Why only
four? I ask. Why not four hundred? I hear she has
been seeking shelter for the homeless. What about my
humble cabins behind the cattle run? They are at
her disposal. And so forth. And so on. Mr. Shui Ta,
do you think Miss Shen Te could be persuaded to
listen to certain ideas of mine? Ideas like these?

SHUI TA: Mr. Shu Fu, she would be honored.

Enter WONG *and the* POLICEMAN. MR. SHU FU *turns
abruptly away and studies the shelves.*

WONG: Is Miss Shen Te here?

SHUI TA: No.

WONG: I am Wong the water seller. You are Mr. Shui Ta?

SHUI TA: I am.

WONG: I am a friend of Shen Te's.

SHUI TA: An intimate friend, I hear.

WONG (*to the* POLICEMAN): You see? (*To* SHUI TA:) It's because of my hand.

POLICEMAN: He hurt his hand, sir, that's a fact.

SHUI TA (*quickly*): You need a sling, I see. (*He takes a shawl from the back room, and throws it to* WONG.)

WONG: But that's her new shawl!

SHUI TA: She has no more use for it.

WONG: But she bought it to please someone!

SHUI TA: It happens to be no longer necessary.

WONG (*making the sling*): She is my only witness.

POLICEMAN: Mr. Shui Ta, your cousin is supposed to have seen the barber hit the water seller with a curling iron.

SHUI TA: I'm afraid my cousin was not present at the time.

WONG: But she was, sir! Just ask her! Isn't she in?

SHUI TA (*gravely*): Mr. Wong, my cousin has her own troubles. You wouldn't wish her to add to them by committing perjury?

WONG: But it was she that told me to go to the judge!

SHUI TA: Was the judge supposed to heal your hand?

> MR. SHU FU *turns quickly around.* SHUI TA *bows to* SHU FU, *and vice versa.*

WONG (*taking the sling off, and putting it back*): I see how it is.

POLICEMAN: Well, I'll be on my way. (*To* WONG:) And you be careful. If Mr. Shu Fu wasn't a man who tempers justice with mercy, as the saying is, you'd be in jail for libel. Be off with you!

> *Exit* WONG, *followed by* POLICEMAN.

SHUI TA: Profound apologies, Mr. Shu Fu.

SHU FU: Not at all, Mr. Shui Ta. (*Pointing to the shawl.*) The episode is over?

SHUI TA: It may take her time to recover. There are some fresh wounds.

SHU FU: We shall be discreet. Delicate. A short vacation could be arranged. . . .

SHUI TA: First of course, you and she would have to talk things over.

SHU FU: At a small supper in a small, but high-class, restaurant.

SHUI TA: I'll go and find her. (*Exit into back room.*)

MRS. SHIN (*sticking her head in again*): Time for congratulations, Mr. Shu Fu?

SHU FU: Ah, Mrs. Shin! Please inform Miss Shen Te's guests they may take shelter in the cabins behind the cattle run!

MRS. SHIN *nods, grinning.*

SHU FU (*to the audience*): Well? What do you think of me, ladies and gentlemen? What could a man do more? Could he be less selfish? More farsighted? A small supper in a small but . . . Does that bring rather vulgar and clumsy thoughts into your mind? Ts, ts, ts. Nothing of the sort will occur. She won't even be touched. Not even accidentally while passing the salt. An exchange of ideas only. Over the flowers on the table—white chrysanthemums, by the way (*he writes down a note of this*)—yes, over the white chrysanthemums, two young souls will . . . shall I say "find each other"? We shall NOT exploit the misfortune of others. Understanding? Yes. An offer of assistance? Certainly. But quietly. Almost inaudibly. Perhaps with a single glance. A glance that could also —also mean more.

MRS. SHIN (*coming forward*): Everything under control, Mr. Shu Fu?

SHU FU: Oh, Mrs. Shin, what do you know about this worthless rascal Yang Sun?

MRS. SHIN: Why, he's the most worthless rascal . . .

SHU FU: Is he really? You're sure? (*As she opens her mouth.*) From now on, he doesn't exist! Can't be found anywhere!

Enter YANG SUN.

YANG SUN: What's been going on here?

MRS. SHIN: Shall I call Mr. Shui Ta, Mr. Shu Fu? He wouldn't want strangers in here!

SHU FU: Mr. Shui Ta is in conference with Miss Shen Te. Not to be disturbed.

YANG SUN: Shen Te here? I didn't see her come in. What kind of conference?

SHU FU (*not letting him enter the back room*): Patience, dear sir! And if by chance I have an inkling who you are, pray take note that Miss Shen Te and I are about to announce our engagement.

YANG SUN: What?

MRS. SHIN: You didn't expect that, did you?

YANG SUN *is trying to push past the barber into the back room when* SHEN TE *comes out.*

SHU FU: My dear Shen Te, ten thousand apologies! Perhaps you . . .

YANG SUN: What is it, Shen Te? Have you gone crazy?

SHEN TE (*breathless*): My cousin and Mr. Shu Fu have come to an understanding. They wish me to hear Mr. Shu Fu's plans for helping the poor.

YANG SUN: Your cousin wants to part us.

SHEN TE: Yes.

YANG SUN: And you've agreed to it?

SHEN TE: Yes.

YANG SUN: They told you I was bad. (SHEN TE *is silent*.) And suppose I am. Does that make me need you less? I'm low, Shen Te, I have no money, I don't do the right thing but at least I put up a fight! (*He is near her now, and speaks in an undertone*.) Have you no eyes? Look at him. Have you forgotten already?

SHEN TE: No.

YANG SUN: How it was raining?

SHEN TE: No.

YANG SUN: How you cut me down from the willow tree? Bought me water? Promised me money to fly with?

SHEN TE (*shakily*): Yang Sun, what do you want?

YANG SUN: I want you to come with me.

SHEN TE (*in a small voice*): Forgive me, Mr. Shu Fu, I want to go with Mr. Yang Sun.

YANG SUN: We're lovers you know. Give me the key to the shop. (SHEN TE *takes the key from around her neck*. YANG SUN *puts it on the counter. To* MRS. SHIN:) Leave it under the mat when you're through. Let's go, Shen Te.

SHU FU: But this is rape! Mr. Shui Ta!!

YANG SUN (*to* SHEN TE): Tell him not to shout.

SHEN TE: Please don't shout for my cousin, Mr. Shu Fu.

He doesn't agree with me, I know, but he's wrong.
(*To the audience*:)

I want to go with the man I love
I don't want to count the cost
I don't want to consider if it's wise
I don't want to know if he loves me
I want to go with the man I love.

YANG SUN: That's the spirit.

And the couple leave.

5a

In front of the inner curtain. SHEN TE *in her wedding clothes, on the way to her wedding.* ˘

SHEN TE: Something terrible has happened. As I left the shop with Yang Sun, I found the old carpet dealer's wife waiting on the street, trembling all over. She told me her husband had taken to his bed sick with all the worry and excitement over the two hundred silver dollars they lent me. She said it would be best if I gave it back now. Of course, I had to say I would. She said she couldn't quite trust my cousin Shui Ta or even my fiancé Yang Sun. There were tears in her eyes. With my emotions in an uproar, I threw myself into Yang Sun's arms, I couldn't resist him. The things he'd said to Shui Ta had taught Shen Te nothing. Sinking into his arms, I said to myself:

To let no one perish, not even oneself
To fill everyone with happiness, even oneself
Is so good

How could I have forgotten those two old people? Yang Sun swept me away like a small hurricane. But he's not a bad man, and he loves me. He'd rather work in the cement factory than owe his flying to a crime. Though, of course, flying *is* a great passion with Sun. Now, on the way to my wedding, I waver between fear and joy.

6

The "private dining room" on the upper floor of a cheap restaurant in a poor section of town. With SHEN TE: *the* GRANDFATHER, *the* SISTER-IN-LAW, *the* NIECE, MRS. SHIN, *the* UNEMPLOYED MAN. *In a corner, alone, a* PRIEST. *A* WAITER *pouring wine. Downstage,* YANG SUN *talking to his* MOTHER. *He wears a dinner jacket.*

YANG SUN: Bad news, Mamma. She came right out and told me she can't sell the shop for me. Some idiot is bringing a claim because he lent her the two hundred she gave you.

MRS. YANG: What did you say? Of course, you can't marry her now.

YANG SUN: It's no use saying anything to *her*. I've sent for her cousin, Mr. Shui Ta. He said there was nothing in writing.

MRS. YANG: Good idea. I'll go and look for him. Keep an eye on things.

Exit MRS. YANG. SHEN TE *has been pouring wine.*

SHEN TE (*to the audience, pitcher in hand*): I wasn't mistaken in him. He's bearing up well. Though it must have been an awful blow—giving up flying. I do love him so. (*Calling across the room to him:*) Sun, you haven't drunk a toast with the bride!

YANG SUN: What do we drink to?

SHEN TE: Why, to the future!

YANG SUN: When the bridegroom's dinner jacket won't be a hired one!

SHEN TE: But when the bride's dress will still get rained on sometimes!

YANG SUN: To everything we ever wished for!

SHEN TE: May all our dreams come true!

They drink.

YANG SUN (*with loud conviviality*): And now, friends, before the wedding gets under way, I have to ask the bride a few questions. I've no idea what kind of wife she'll make, and it worries me. (*Wheeling on* SHEN TE.) For example. Can you make five cups of tea with three tea leaves?

SHEN TE: No.

YANG SUN: So I won't be getting very much tea. Can you sleep on a straw mattress the size of that book? (*He points to the large volume the* PRIEST *is reading.*)

SHEN TE: The two of us?

YANG SUN: The one of you.

SHEN TE: In that case, no.

YANG SUN: What a wife! I'm shocked!

While the audience is laughing, his MOTHER *returns. With a shrug of her shoulders, she tells* YANG SUN *the expected guest hasn't arrived. The* PRIEST *shuts the book with a bang, and makes for the door.*

MRS. YANG: Where are *you* off to? It's only a matter of minutes.

PRIEST (*watch in hand*): Time goes on, Mrs. Yang, and I've another wedding to attend to. Also a funeral.

MRS. YANG (*irately*): D'you think we planned it this way? I was hoping to manage with one pitcher of wine, and we've run through two already. (*Points to empty pitcher. Loudly.*) My dear Shen Te, I don't know where your cousin can be keeping himself!

SHEN TE: My cousin?!

MRS. YANG: Certainly. I'm old-fashioned enough to think such a close relative should attend the wedding.

SHEN TE: Oh, Sun, is it the three hundred silver dollars?

YANG SUN (*not looking her in the eye*): Are you deaf? Mother says she's old-fashioned. And I say I'm considerate. We'll wait another fifteen minutes.

HUSBAND: Another fifteen minutes.

MRS. YANG (*addressing the company*): Now you all know, don't you, that my son is getting a job as a mail pilot?

SISTER-IN-LAW: In Peking, too, isn't it?

MRS. YANG: In Peking, too! The two of us are moving to Peking!

SHEN TE: Sun, tell your mother Peking is out of the question now.

YANG SUN: Your cousin'll tell her. If he agrees. I don't agree.

SHEN TE (*amazed, and dismayed*): Sun!

YANG SUN: I hate this godforsaken Setzuan. What people! Know what they look like when I half close my eyes? Horses! Whinnying, fretting, stamping, screwing their necks up! (*Loudly.*) And what is it the thunder says? They are su-per-flu-ous! (*He hammers out the syllables.*) They've run their last race! They can go trample themselves to death! (*Pause.*) I've got to get out of here.

SHEN TE: But I've promised the money to the old couple.

YANG SUN: And since you always do the wrong thing, it's lucky your cousin's coming. Have another drink.

SHEN TE (*quietly*): My cousin can't be coming.

YANG SUN: How d'you mean?

SHEN TE: My cousin can't be where I am.

YANG SUN: Quite a conundrum!

SHEN TE (*desperately*): Sun, I'm the one that loves you. Not my cousin. He was thinking of the job in Peking when he promised you the old couple's money—

YANG SUN: Right. And that's why he's bringing the three hundred silver dollars. Here—to my wedding.

SHEN TE: He is not bringing the three hundred silver dollars.

YANG SUN: Huh? What makes you think that?

SHEN TE (*looking into his eyes*): He says you only bought one ticket to Peking.

Short pause.

YANG SUN: That was yesterday. (*He pulls two tickets part way out of his inside pocket, making her look under his coat.*) Two tickets. I don't want Mother to know. She'll get left behind. I sold her furniture to buy these tickets, so you see . . .

SHEN TE: But what's to become of the old couple?

YANG SUN: What's to become of me? Have another drink. Or do you believe in moderation? If I drink, I fly again. And if you drink, you may learn to understand me.

SHEN TE: You want to fly. But I can't help you.

YANG SUN: "Here's a plane, my darling—but it's only got one wing!"

The WAITER *enters.*

WAITER: Mrs. Yang!

MRS. YANG: Yes?

WAITER: Another pitcher of wine, ma'am?

MRS. YANG: We have enough, thanks. Drinking makes me sweat.

WAITER: Would you mind paying, ma'am?

MRS. YANG (*to everyone*): Just be patient a few moments

longer, everyone, Mr. Shui Ta is on his way over! (*To the* WAITER:) Don't be a spoilsport.

WAITER: I can't let you leave till you've paid your bill, ma'am.

MRS. YANG: But they know me here!

WAITER: That's just it.

PRIEST (*ponderously getting up*): I humbly take my leave. (*And he does.*)

MRS. YANG (*to the others, desperately*): Stay where you are, everybody! The priest says he'll be back in two minutes!

YANG SUN: It's no good, Mamma. Ladies and gentlemen, Mr. Shui Ta still hasn't arrived and the priest has gone home. We won't detain you any longer.

They are leaving now.

GRANDFATHER (*in the doorway, having forgotten to put his glass down*): To the bride! (*He drinks, puts down the glass, and follows the others.*)

Pause.

SHEN TE: Shall I go too?

YANG SUN: You? Aren't you the bride? Isn't this your wedding? (*He drags her across the room, tearing her wedding dress.*) If we can wait, you can wait. Mother calls me her falcon. She wants to see me in the clouds. But I think it may be St. Nevercome's Day before she'll go to the door and see my plane thunder by. (*Pause. He pretends the guests are still present.*) Why such a lull in the conversation, ladies and gentlemen? Don't you like it here? The ceremony is only slightly postponed—because an important guest is expected at any moment. Also because the bride doesn't know what love is. While we're waiting, the bridegroom will sing a little song. (*He does so.*)

THE SONG OF ST. NEVERCOME'S DAY

On a certain day, as is generally known,
    One and all will be shouting: Hooray, hooray!
For the beggar maid's son has a solid-gold throne
    And the day is St. Nevercome's Day
On St. Nevercome's, Nevercome's, Nevercome's Day
    He'll sit on his solid-gold throne

Oh, hooray, hooray! That day goodness will pay!
    That day badness will cost you your head!
And merit and money will smile and be funny
    While exchanging salt and bread
On St. Nevercome's, Nevercome's, Nevercome's Day
    While exchanging salt and bread

And the grass, oh, the grass will look down at the sky
    And the pebbles will roll up the stream
And all men will be good without batting an eye
    They will make of our earth a dream
On St. Nevercome's, Nevercome's, Nevercome's Day
    They will make of our earth a dream

And as for me, that's the day I shall be
    A flyer and one of the best
Unemployed man, you will have work to do
    Washerwoman, you'll get your rest
On St. Nevercome's, Nevercome's, Nevercome's Day
    Washerwoman, you'll get your rest

MRS. YANG: It looks like he's not coming.

The three of them sit looking at the door.

*Wong's den. The sewer pipe is again transparent and again
the* GODS *appear to* WONG *in a dream.*

WONG: I'm so glad you've come, illustrious ones. It's Shen
Te. She's in great trouble from following the rule
about loving thy neighbor. Perhaps she's *too* good for
this world!

FIRST GOD: Nonsense! You are eaten up by lice and
doubts!

WONG: Forgive me, illustrious one, I only meant you might
deign to intervene.

FIRST GOD: Out of the question! My colleague here inter-
vened in some squabble or other only yesterday. (*He
points to the* THIRD GOD *who has a black eye.*) The
results are before us!

WONG: She had to call on her cousin again. But not even
he could help. I'm afraid the shop is done for.

THIRD GOD (*a little concerned*): Perhaps we should help
after all?

FIRST GOD: The gods help those that help themselves.

WONG: What if we *can't* help ourselves, illustrious ones?

Slight pause.

SECOND GOD: Try, anyway! Suffering ennobles!

FIRST GOD: Our faith in Shen Te is unshaken!

THIRD GOD: We certainly haven't found any *other* good people. You can see where we spend our nights from the straw on our clothes.

WONG: You might help her find her way by—

FIRST GOD: The good man finds his own way here below!

SECOND GOD: The good woman too.

FIRST GOD: The heavier the burden, the greater her strength!

THIRD GOD: We're only onlookers, you know.

FIRST GOD: And everything will be all right in the end, O ye of little faith!

They are gradually disappearing through these last lines.

7

The yard behind Shen Te's shop. A few articles of furniture on a cart. SHEN TE *and* MRS. SHIN *are taking the washing off the line.*

MRS. SHIN: If you ask me, you should fight tooth and nail to keep the shop.

SHEN TE: How can I? I have to sell the tobacco to pay back the two hundred silver dollars today.

MRS. SHIN: No husband, no tobacco, no house and home! What are you going to live on?

SHEN TE: I can work. I can sort tobacco.

MRS. SHIN: Hey, look, Mr. Shui Ta's trousers! He must have left here stark naked!

SHEN TE: Oh, he may have another pair, Mrs. Shin.

MRS. SHIN: But if he's gone for good as you say, why has he left his pants behind?

SHEN TE: Maybe he's thrown them away.

MRS. SHIN: Can I take them?

SHEN TE: Oh, no.

Enter MR. SHU FU, *running.*

SHU FU: Not a word! Total silence! I know all. You have

sacrificed your own love and happiness so as not to hurt a dear old couple who had put their trust in you! Not in vain does this district—for all its malevolent tongues—call you the Angel of the Slums! That young man couldn't rise to your level, so you left him. And now, when I see you closing up the little shop, that veritable haven of rest for the multitude, well, I cannot, I cannot let it pass. Morning after morning I have stood watching in the doorway not unmoved—while you graciously handed out rice to the wretched. Is that never to happen again? Is the good woman of Setzuan to disappear? If only you would allow *me* to assist you! Now don't say anything! No assurances, no exclamations of gratitude! (*He has taken out his checkbook.*) Here! A blank check. (*He places it on the cart.*) Just my signature. Fill it out as you wish. Any sum in the world. I herewith retire from the scene, quietly, unobtrusively, making no claims, on tiptoe, full of veneration, absolutely selflessly . . . (*He has gone.*)

MRS. SHIN: Well! You're saved. There's always some idiot of a man. . . . Now hurry! Put down a thousand silver dollars and let me fly to the bank before he comes to his senses.

SHEN TE: I can pay you for the washing without any check.

MRS. SHIN: What? You're not going to cash it just because you might have to marry him? Are you crazy? Men like him *want* to be led by the nose! Are you still thinking of that flyer? All Yellow Street knows how he treated you!

SHEN TE:

When I heard his cunning laugh, I was afraid

But when I saw the holes in his shoes, I loved him
dearly.

MRS. SHIN: Defending that good-for-nothing after all that's
happened!

SHEN TE (*staggering as she holds some of the washing*):
Oh!

MRS. SHIN (*taking the washing from her, dryly*): So you
feel dizzy when you stretch and bend? There couldn't
be a little visitor on the way? If that's it, you can forget Mr. Shu Fu's blank check: it wasn't meant for a
christening present!

She goes to the back with a basket. SHEN TE'*s eyes
follow* MRS. SHIN *for a moment. Then she looks down
at her own body, feels her stomach, and a great joy
comes into her eyes.*

SHEN TE: O joy! A new human being is on the way. The
world awaits him. In the cities the people say: he's
got to be reckoned with, this new human being! (*She
imagines a little boy to be present, and introduces him
to the audience.*) This is my son, the well-known
flyer!

Say: Welcome
To the conqueror of unknown mountains and
        unreachable regions
Who brings us our mail across the impassable deserts!

She leads him up and down by the hand.

Take a look at the world, my son. That's a tree. Tree,
yes. Say: "Hello, tree!" And bow. Like this. (*She
bows.*) Now you know each other. And, look, here
comes the water seller. He's a friend, give him your

hand. A cup of fresh water for my little son, please. Yes, it *is* a warm day. (*Handing the cup.*) Oh dear, a policeman, we'll have to make a circle round *him*. Perhaps we can pick a few cherries over there in the rich Mr. Pung's garden. But we mustn't be seen. You want cherries? Just like children with fathers. No, no, you can't go straight at them like that. Don't pull. We must learn to be reasonable. Well, have it your own way. (*She has let him make for the cherries.*) Can you reach? Where to put them? Your mouth is the best place. (*She tries one herself.*) Mmm, they're good. But the policeman, we must run! (*They run.*) Yes, back to the street. Calm now, so no one will notice us. (*Walking the street with her child, she sings.*)

> Once a plum—'twas in Japan—
> Made a conquest of a man
> But the man's turn soon did come
> For he gobbled up the plum

Enter WONG, *with a* CHILD *by the hand. He coughs.*

SHEN TE: Wong!

WONG: It's about the carpenter, Shen Te. He's lost his shop, and he's been drinking. His children are on the streets. This is one. Can you help?

SHEN TE (*to the* CHILD): Come here, little man. (*Takes him down to the footlights. To the audience:*)

> You there! A man is asking you for shelter!
> A man of tomorrow says: what about today?
> His friend the conqueror, whom you know,
> Is his advocate!

(*To* WONG:) He can live in Mr. Shu Fu's cabins. I may have to go there myself. I'm going to have a baby. That's a secret—don't tell Yang Sun—we'd only be in his way. Can you find the carpenter for me?

WONG: I knew you'd think of something. (*To the* CHILD:) Good-bye, son, I'm going for your father.

SHEN TE: What about your hand, Wong? I wanted to help, but my cousin . . .

WONG: Oh, I can get along with one hand, don't worry. (*He shows how he can handle his pole with his left hand alone.*)

SHEN TE: But your right hand! Look, take this cart, sell everything that's on it, and go to the doctor with the money . . .

WONG: She's still good. But first I'll bring the carpenter. I'll pick up the cart when I get back. (*Exit* WONG.)

SHEN TE (*to the* CHILD): Sit down over here, son, till your father comes.

The CHILD *sits cross-legged on the ground. Enter the* HUSBAND *and* WIFE, *each dragging a large, full sack.*

WIFE (*furtively*): You're alone, Shen Te, dear?

SHEN TE *nods. The* WIFE *beckons to the* NEPHEW *offstage. He comes on with another sack.*

WIFE: Your cousin's away? (SHEN TE *nods.*) He's not coming back?

SHEN TE: No. I'm giving up the shop.

WIFE: That's why we're here. We want to know if we can

leave these things in your new home. Will you do us this favor?

SHEN TE: Why, yes, I'd be glad to.

HUSBAND (*cryptically*): And if anyone asks about them, say they're yours.

SHEN TE: Would anyone ask?

WIFE (*with a glance back at her husband*): Oh, someone might. The police, for instance. They don't seem to like us. Where can we put it?

SHEN TE: Well, I'd rather not get in any more trouble . . .

WIFE: Listen to her! The good woman of Setzuan!

SHEN TE *is silent.*

HUSBAND: There's enough tobacco in those sacks to give us a new start in life. We could have our own tobacco factory!

SHEN TE (*slowly*): You'll have to put them in the back room.

The sacks are taken off-stage, while the CHILD *is alone. Shyly glancing about him, he goes to the garbage can, starts playing with the contents, and eating some of the scraps. The others return.*

WIFE: We're countng on you, Shen Te!

SHEN TE: Yes. (*She sees the* CHILD *and is shocked.*)

HUSBAND: We'll see you in Mr. Shu Fu's cabins.

NEPHEW: The day after tomorrow.

SHEN TE: Yes. Now, go. Go! I'm not feeling well.

Exeunt all three, virtually pushed off.

> He is eating the refuse in the garbage can!
> Only look at his little gray mouth!

Pause. Music.

> As this is the world *my* son will enter
> I will study to defend him.
> To be good to you, my son,
> I shall be a tigress to all others
> If I have to.
> And I shall have to.

She starts to go.

> One more time, then. I hope really the last.

Exit SHEN TE, taking Shui Ta's trousers. MRS. SHIN enters and watches her with marked interest. Enter the SISTER-IN-LAW and the GRANDFATHER.

SISTER-IN-LAW: So it's true, the shop has closed down. And the furniture's in the back yard. It's the end of the road!

MRS. SHIN (*pompously*): The fruit of high living, selfishness, and sensuality! Down the primrose path to Mr. Shu Fu's cabins—with you!

SISTER-IN-LAW: Cabins? Rat holes! He gave them to us because his soap supplies only went moldy there!

Enter the UNEMPLOYED MAN.

UNEMPLOYED MAN: Shen Te is moving?

SISTER-IN-LAW: Yes. She was sneaking away.

MRS. SHIN: She's ashamed of herself, and no wonder!

UNEMPLOYED MAN: Tell her to call Mr. Shui Ta or she's done for this time!

SISTER-IN-LAW: Tell her to call Mr. Shui Ta or *we're* done for this time.

Enter WONG *and* CARPENTER, *the latter with a* CHILD *on each hand.*

CARPENTER: So we'll have a roof over our heads for a change!

MRS. SHIN: Roof? Whose roof?

CARPENTER: Mr. Shu Fu's cabins. And we have little Feng to thank for it. (FENG, *we find, is the name of the* CHILD *already there; his* FATHER *now takes him. To the other two*:) Bow to your little brother, you two!

The CARPENTER *and the two new arrivals bow to* FENG. *Enter* SHUI TA.

UNEMPLOYED MAN: Sst! Mr. Shui Ta!

Pause.

SHUI TA: And what is this crowd here for, may I ask?

WONG: How do you do, Mr. Shui Ta. This is the carpenter. Miss Shen Te promised him space in Mr. Shu Fu's cabins.

SHUI TA: That will not be possible.

CARPENTER: We can't go there after all?

SHUI TA: All the space is needed for other purposes.

SISTER-IN-LAW: You mean we have to get out? But we've got nowhere to go.

SHUI TA: Miss Shen Te finds it possible to provide employment. If the proposition interests you, you may stay in the cabins.

SISTER-IN-LAW (*with distaste*): You mean *work*? Work for Miss Shen Te?

SHUI TA: Making tobacco, yes. There are three bales here already. Would you like to get them?

SISTER-IN-LAW (*trying to bluster*): We have our own tobacco! We were in the tobacco business before you were born!

SHUI TA (*to the* CARPENTER *and the* UNEMPLOYED MAN): You *don't* have your own tobacco. What about you?

The CARPENTER *and the* UNEMPLOYED MAN *get the point, and go for the sacks. Enter* MRS. MI TZU.

MRS. MI TZU: Mr. Shui Ta? I've brought you your three hundred silver dollars.

SHUI TA: I'll sign your lease instead. I've decided not to sell.

MRS. MI TZU: What? You don't need the money for that flyer?

SHUI TA: No.

MRS. MI TZU: And you can pay six months' rent?

SHUI TA (*takes the barber's blank check from the cart and fills it out*): Here is a check for ten thousand silver dollars. On Mr. Shu Fu's account. Look! (*He shows her the signature on the check.*) Your six months' rent will be in your hands by seven this evening. And now, if you'll excuse me.

MRS. MI TZU: So it's Mr. Shu Fu now. The flyer has been given his walking papers. These modern girls! In my day they'd have said she was flighty. That poor, deserted Mr. Yang Sun!

Exit MRS. MI TZU. *The* CARPENTER *and the* UNEMPLOYED MAN *drag the three sacks back on the stage.*

CARPENTER (*to* SHUI TA): I don't know why I'm doing this for you.

SHUI TA: Perhaps your children want to eat, Mr. Carpenter.

SISTER-IN-LAW (*catching sight of the sacks*): Was my brother-in-law here?

MRS. SHIN: Yes, he was.

SISTER-IN-LAW: I thought as much. I know those sacks! That's our tobacco!

SHUI TA: Really? I thought it came from my back room! Shall we consult the police on the point?

SISTER-IN-LAW (*defeated*): No.

SHUI TA: Perhaps you will show me the way to Mr. Shu Fu's cabins?

Taking FENG *by the hand,* SHUI TA *goes off, followed by the* CARPENTER *and his two older children, the* SISTER-IN-LAW, *the* GRANDFATHER, *and the* UNEMPLOYED MAN. *Each of the last three drags a sack. Enter* OLD MAN *and* OLD WOMAN.

MRS. SHIN: A pair of pants—missing from the clothesline one minute—and next minute on the honorable backside of Mr. Shui Ta.

OLD WOMAN: We thought Miss Shen Te was here.

MRS. SHIN (*preoccupied*): Well, she's not.

OLD MAN: There was something she was going to give us.

WONG: She was going to help me too. (*Looking at his hand.*) It'll be too late soon. But she'll be back. This cousin has never stayed long.

MRS. SHIN (*approaching a conclusion*): No, he hasn't, has he?

7a

The Sewer Pipe: WONG *asleep. In his dream, he tells the* GODS *his fears. The* GODS *seem tired from all their travels. They stop for a moment and look over their shoulders at the water seller.*

WONG: Illustrious ones. I've been having a bad dream. Our beloved Shen Te was in great distress in the rushes down by the river—the spot where the bodies of suicides are washed up. She kept staggering and holding her head down as if she was carrying something and it was dragging her down into the mud. When I called out to her, she said she had to take your Book of Rules to the other side, and not get it wet, or the ink would all come off. You had talked to her about the virtues, you know, the time she gave you shelter in Setzuan.

THIRD GOD: Well, but what do you suggest, my dear Wong?

WONG: Maybe a little relaxation of the rules, Benevolent One, in view of the bad times.

THIRD GOD: As for instance?

WONG: Well, um, good will, for instance, might do instead of love?

THIRD GOD: I'm afraid that would create new problems.

WONG: Or, instead of justice, good sportsmanship?

THIRD GOD: That would only mean more work.

WONG: Instead of honor, outward propriety?

THIRD GOD: Still more work! No, no! The rules will have to stand, my dear Wong!

Wearily shaking their heads, all three journey on.

8

*Shui Ta's tobacco factory in Shu Fu's cabins. Huddled to-
gether behind bars, several families, mostly women and
children. Among these people the* SISTER-IN-LAW, *the*
GRANDFATHER, *the* CARPENTER, *and his* THREE CHILDREN.
Enter MRS. YANG *followed by* YANG SUN.

MRS. YANG (*to the audience*): There's something I just
have to tell you: strength and wisdom are wonderful
things. The strong and wise Mr. Shui Ta has trans-
formed my son from a dissipated good-for-nothing
into a model citizen. As you may have heard, Mr.
Shui Ta opened a small tobacco factory near the cattle
runs. It flourished. Three months ago—I shall never
forget it—I asked for an appointment, and Mr. Shui
Ta agreed to see us—me and my son. I can see him
now as he came through the door to meet us. . . .

Enter SHUI TA *from a door.*

SHUI TA: What can I do for you, Mrs. Yang?

MRS. YANG: This morning the police came to the house.
We find you've brought an action for breach of promise of marriage. In the name of Shen Te. You also
claim that Sun came by two hundred silver dollars by
improper means.

SHUI TA: That is correct.

MRS. YANG: Mr. Shui Ta, the money's all gone. When the
Peking job didn't materialize, he ran through it all in

three days. I know he's a good-for-nothing. He sold my furniture. He was moving to Peking without me. Miss Shen Te thought highly of him at one time.

SHUI TA: What do *you* say, Mr. Yang Sun?

YANG SUN: The money's gone.

SHUI TA (*to* MRS. YANG): Mrs. Yang, in consideration of my cousin's incomprehensible weakness for your son, I am prepared to give him another chance. He can have a job—here. The two hundred silver dollars will be taken out of his wages.

YANG SUN: So it's the factory or jail?

SHUI TA: Take your choice.

YANG SUN: May I speak with Shen Te?

SHUI TA: You may not.

Pause.

YANG SUN (*sullenly*): Show me where to go.

MRS. YANG: Mr. Shui Ta, you are kindness itself: the gods will reward you! (*To* YANG SUN:) And honest work will make a man of you, my boy. (YANG SUN *follows* SHUI TA *into the factory.* MRS. YANG *comes down again to the footlights.*) Actually, honest work didn't agree with him—at first. And he got no opportunity to distinguish himself till—in the third week—when the wages were being paid . . .

SHUI TA *has a bag of money. Standing next to his foreman—the former* UNEMPLOYED MAN—*he counts out the wages. It is* YANG SUN's *turn.*

UNEMPLOYED MAN (*reading*): Carpenter, six silver dollars. Yang Sun, six silver dollars.

YANG SUN (*quietly*): Excuse me, sir. I don't think it can be more than five. May I see? (*He takes the foreman's list.*) It says six working days. But that's a mistake, sir. I took a day off for court business. And I won't take what I haven't earned, however miserable the pay is!

UNEMPLOYED MAN: Yang Sun. Five silver dollars. (*To* SHUI TA:) A rare case, Mr. Shui Ta!

SHUI TA: How is it the book says six when it should say five?

UNEMPLOYED MAN: I must've made a mistake, Mr. Shui Ta. (*With a look at* YANG SUN.) It won't happen again.

SHUI TA (*taking* YANG SUN *aside*): You don't hold back, do you? You give your all to the firm. You're even honest. Do the foreman's mistakes always favor the workers?

YANG SUN: He does have . . . friends.

SHUI TA: Thank you. May I offer you any little recompense?

YANG SUN: Give me a trial period of one week, and I'll prove my intelligence is worth more to you than my strength.

MRS. YANG (*still down at the footlights*): Fighting words, fighting words! That evening, I said to Sun: "If you're a flyer, then fly, my falcon! Rise in the world!" And he got to be foreman. Yes, in Mr. Shui Ta's tobacco factory, he worked real miracles.

We see YANG SUN *with his legs apart standing behind the workers who are handing along a basket of raw tobacco above their heads.*

YANG SUN: Faster! Faster! You, there, d'you think you can just stand around, now you're not foreman any more? It'll be your job to lead us in song. Sing!

UNEMPLOYED MAN *starts singing. The others join in the refrain.*

SONG OF THE EIGHTH ELEPHANT

Chang had seven elephants—all much the same—
    But then there was Little Brother
The seven, they were wild, Little Brother, he was tame
    And to guard them Chang chose Little Brother
        Run faster!
        Mr. Chang has a forest park
        Which must be cleared before tonight
        And already it's growing dark!

When the seven elephants cleared that forest park
    Mr. Chang rode high on Little Brother
While the seven toiled and moiled till dark
    On his big behind sat Little Brother
        Dig faster!
        Mr. Chang has a forest park
        Which must be cleared before tonight
        And already it's growing dark!

And the seven elephants worked many an hour
    Till none of them could work another
Old Chang, he looked sour, on the seven he did glower
    But gave a pound of rice to Little Brother

What was that?
Mr. Chang has a forest park
Which must be cleared before tonight
And already it's growing dark!

And the seven elephants hadn't any tusks
The one that had the tusks was Little Brother
Seven are no match for one, if the one has a gun!
How old Chang did laugh at Little Brother!
Keep on digging!
Mr. Chang has a forest park
Which must be cleared before tonight
And already it's growing dark!

Smoking a cigar, SHUI TA *strolls by.* YANG SUN, *laughing, has joined in the refrain of the third stanza and speeded up the tempo of the last stanza by clapping his hands.*

MRS. YANG: And that's why I say: strength and wisdom are wonderful things. It took the strong and wise Mr. Shui Ta to bring out the best in Yang Sun. A real superior man is like a bell. If you ring it, it rings, and if you don't, it don't, as the saying is.

9

Shen Te's shop, now an office with club chairs and fine carpets. It is raining. SHUI TA, *now fat, is just dismissing the* OLD MAN *and* OLD WOMAN. MRS. SHIN, *in obviously new clothes, looks on, smirking.*

SHUI TA: No! I can NOT tell you when we expect her back.

OLD WOMAN: The two hundred silver dollars came today. In an envelope. There was no letter, but it must be from Shen Te. We want to write and thank her. May we have her address?

SHUI TA: I'm afraid I haven't got it.

OLD MAN (*pulling* OLD WOMAN's *sleeve*): Let's be going.

OLD WOMAN: She's got to come back some time!

They move off, uncertainly, worried. SHUI TA *bows.*

MRS. SHIN: They lost the carpet shop because they couldn't pay their taxes. The money arrived too late.

SHUI TA: They could have come to me.

MRS. SHIN: People don't like coming to you.

SHUI TA (*sits suddenly, one hand to his head*): I'm dizzy.

MRS. SHIN: After all, you *are* in your seventh month. But old Mrs. Shin will be there in your hour of trial! (*She cackles feebly.*)

117

SHUI TA (*in a stifled voice*): Can I count on that?

MRS. SHIN: We all have our price, and mine won't be too high for the great Mr. Shui Ta! (*She opens* SHUI TA's *collar.*)

SHUI TA: It's for the child's sake. All of this.

MRS. SHIN: "All for the child," of course.

SHUI TA: I'm so fat. People must notice.

MRS. SHIN: Oh no, they think it's 'cause you're rich.

SHUI TA (*more feelingly*): What will happen to the child?

MRS. SHIN: You ask that nine times a day. Why, it'll have the best that money can buy!

SHUI TA: He must never see Shui Ta.

MRS. SHIN: Oh, no. Always Shen Te.

SHUI TA: What about the neighbors? There are rumors, aren't there?

MRS. SHIN: As long as Mr. Shu Fu doesn't find out, there's nothing to worry about. Drink this.

Enter YANG SUN *in a smart business suit, and carrying a businessman's briefcase.* SHUI TA *is more or less in* MRS. SHIN's *arms.*

YANG SUN (*surprised*): I guess I'm in the way.

SHUI TA (*ignoring this, rises with an effort*): Till tomorrow, Mrs. Shin.

MRS. SHIN *leaves with a smile, putting her new gloves on.*

YANG SUN: Gloves now! She couldn't be fleecing you? And since when did *you* have a private life? (*Taking a paper from the briefcase.*) You haven't been at your desk lately, and things are getting out of hand. The police want to close us down. They say that at the most they can only permit twice the lawful number of workers.

SHUI TA (*evasively*): The cabins are quite good enough.

YANG SUN: For the workers maybe, not for the tobacco. They're too damp. We must take over some of Mrs. Mi Tzu's buildings.

SHUI TA: Her price is double what I can pay.

YANG SUN: Not unconditionally. If she has me to stroke her knees she'll come down.

SHUI TA: I'll never agree to that.

YANG SUN: What's wrong? Is it the rain? You get so irritable whenever it rains.

SHUI TA: Never! I will never . . .

YANG SUN: Mrs. Mi Tzu'll be here in five minutes. *You* fix it. And Shu Fu will be with her. . . . What's all that noise?

During the above dialogue, WONG *is heard off-stage, calling:* "The good Shen Te, where is she? Which of you has seen Shen Te, good people? Where is Shen Te?" *A knock. Enter* WONG.

WONG: Mr. Shui Ta, I've come to ask when Miss Shen Te will be back, it's six months now. . . . There are rumors. People say something's happened to her.

SHUI TA: I'm busy. Come back next week.

WONG (*excited*): In the morning there was always rice on her doorstep—for the needy. It's been there again lately!

SHUI TA: And what do people conclude from this?

WONG: That Shen Te is still in Setzuan! She's been . . . (*He breaks off.*)

SHUI TA: She's been what? Mr. Wong, if you're Shen Te's friend, talk a little less about her, that's my advice to you.

WONG: I don't want your advice! Before she disappeared, Miss Shen Te told me something very important— she's pregnant!

YANG SUN: What? What was that?

SHUI TA (*quickly*): The man is lying.

WONG: A good woman isn't so easily forgotten, Mr. Shui Ta.

He leaves. SHUI TA *goes quickly into the back room.*

YANG SUN (*to the audience*): Shen Te pregnant? So that's why. Her cousin sent her away, so I wouldn't get wind of it. I have a son, a Yang appears on the scene, and what happens? Mother and child vanish into thin air! That scoundrel, that unspeakable . . . (*The sound of sobbing is heard from the back room.*) What was that? Someone sobbing? Who was it? Mr. Shui Ta the Tobacco King doesn't weep his heart out. And where does the rice come from that's on the doorstep in the morning? (SHUI TA *returns. He goes to the door and looks out into the rain.*) Where is she?

SHUI TA: Sh! It's nine o'clock. But the rain's so heavy, you can't hear a thing.

YANG SUN: What do you want to hear?

SHUI TA: The mail plane.

YANG SUN: What?!

SHUI TA: I've been told *you* wanted to fly at one time. Is that all forgotten?

YANG SUN: Flying mail is night work. I prefer the daytime. And the firm is very dear to me—after all it belongs to my ex-fiancée, even if she's not around. And she's not, is she?

SHUI TA: What do you mean by that?

YANG SUN: Oh, well, let's say I haven't altogether—lost interest.

SHUI TA: My cousin might like to know that.

YANG SUN: I might not be indifferent—if I found she was being kept under lock and key.

SHUI TA: By whom?

YANG SUN: By you.

SHUI TA: What could you do about it?

YANG SUN: I could submit for discussion—my position in the firm.

SHUI TA: You are now my manager. In return for a more . . . appropriate position, you might agree to drop the inquiry into your ex-fiancée's whereabouts?

YANG SUN: I might.

SHUI TA: What position *would* be more appropriate?

YANG SUN: The one at the top.

SHUI TA: My own? (*Silence.*) And if I preferred to throw you out on your neck?

YANG SUN: I'd come back on my feet. With suitable escort.

SHUI TA: The police?

YANG SUN: The police.

SHUI TA: And when the police found no one?

YANG SUN: I might ask them not to overlook the back room. (*Ending the pretense.*) In short, Mr. Shui Ta, my interest in this young woman has not been officially terminated. I should like to see more of her. (*Into* SHUI TA'*s face:*) Besides, she's pregnant and needs a friend. (*He moves to the door.*) I shall talk about it with the water seller.

Exit. SHUI TA *is rigid for a moment, then he quickly goes into the back room. He returns with Shen Te's belongings: underwear, etc. He takes a long look at the shawl of the previous scene. He then wraps the things in a bundle, which, upon hearing a noise, he hides under the table. Enter* MRS. MI TZU *and* MR. SHU FU. *They put away their umbrellas and galoshes.*

MRS. MI TZU: I thought your manager was here, Mr. Shui Ta. He combines charm with business in a way that can only be to the advantage of all of us.

SHU FU: You sent for us, Mr. Shui Ta?

SHUI TA: The factory is in trouble.

SHU FU: It always is.

SHUI TA: The police are threatening to close us down unless I can show that the extension of our facilities is imminent.

SHU FU: Shui Ta, I'm sick and tired of your constantly expanding projects. I place cabins at your cousin's disposal; you make a factory of them. I hand your cousin a check; you present it. Your cousin disappears; you find the cabins too small and start talking of yet more—

SHUI TA: Mr. Shu Fu, I'm authorized to inform you that Miss Shen Te's return is now imminent.

SHU FU: Imminent? It's becoming his favorite word.

MRS. MI TZU: Yes, what does it mean?

SHUI TA: Mrs. Mi Tzu, I can pay you exactly half what you asked for your buildings. Are you ready to inform the police that I am taking them over?

MRS MI TZU: Certainly, if I can take over your manager.

SHU FU: What?

MRS. MI TZU: He's so efficient.

SHUI TA: I'm afraid I need Mr. Yang Sun.

MRS. MI TZU: So do I.

SHUI TA: He will call on you tomorrow.

SHU FU: So much the better. With Shen Te likely to turn up at any moment, the presence of that young man is hardly in good taste.

SHUI TA: So we have reached a settlement. In what was once the good Shen Te's little shop we are laying the foundations for the great Mr. Shui Ta's twelve magnificent super tobacco markets. You will bear in mind that though they call me the Tobacco King of Setzuan, it is my cousin's interests that have been served . . .

VOICES (*off*): The police, the police! Going to the tobacco shop! Something must have happened!

Enter YANG SUN, WONG *and the* POLICEMAN.

POLICEMAN: Quiet there, quiet, quiet! (*They quiet down.*) I'm sorry, Mr. Shui Ta, but there's a report that you've been depriving Miss Shen Te of her freedom. Not that I believe all I hear, but the whole city's in an uproar.

SHUI TA: That's a lie.

POLICEMAN: Mr. Yang Sun has testified that he heard someone sobbing in the back room.

SHU FU: Mrs. Mi Tzu and myself will testify that no one here has been sobbing.

MRS. MI TZU: We have been quietly smoking our cigars.

POLICEMAN: Mr. Shui Ta, I'm afraid I shall have to take a look at that room. (*He does so. The room is empty.*) No one there, of course, sir.

YANG SUN: But I heard sobbing. What's that? (*He finds the clothes.*)

WONG: Those are Shen Te's things. (*To crowd:*) Shen Te's clothes are here!

VOICES (*off, in sequence*):

—Shen Te's clothes!
—They've been found under the table!
—Body of murdered girl still missing!
—Tobacco King suspected!

POLICEMAN: Mr. Shui Ta, unless you can tell us where the girl is, I'll have to ask you to come along.

SHUI TA: I do not know.

POLICEMAN: I can't say how sorry I am, Mr. Shui Ta. (*He shows him the door.*)

SHUI TA: Everything will be cleared up in no time. There are still judges in Setzuan.

YANG SUN: I heard sobbing!

Wong's den. For the last time, the GODS *appear to the water seller in his dream. They have changed and show signs of a long journey, extreme fatigue, and plenty of mishaps. The* FIRST *no longer has a hat; the* THIRD *has lost a leg; all three are barefoot.*

WONG: Illustrious ones, at last you're here. Shen Te's been gone for months and today her cousin's been arrested. They think he murdered her to get the shop. But I had a dream and in this dream Shen Te said her cousin was keeping her prisoner. You must find her for us, illustrious ones!

FIRST GOD: We've found very few good people anywhere, and even they didn't keep it up. Shen Te is still the only one that stayed good.

SECOND GOD: If she *has* stayed good.

WONG: Certainly she has. But she's vanished.

FIRST GOD: That's the last straw. All is lost!

SECOND GOD: A little moderation, dear colleague!

FIRST GOD (*plaintively*): What's the good of moderation now? If she can't be found, we'll have to resign! The world is a terrible place! Nothing but misery, vulgarity, and waste! Even the countryside isn't what it used to be. The trees are getting their heads chopped off by telephone wires, and there's such a noise from all the gunfire, and I can't stand those heavy clouds of smoke, and—

THIRD GOD: The place is absolutely unlivable! Good intentions bring people to the brink of the abyss, and good deeds push them over the edge. I'm afraid our book of rules is destined for the scrap heap—

SECOND GOD: It's people! They're a worthless lot!

THIRD GOD: The world is too cold!

SECOND GOD: It's people! They're too weak!

FIRST GOD: Dignity, dear colleagues, dignity! Never despair! As for this world, didn't we agree that we only have to find one human being who can stand the place? Well, we found her. True, we lost her again. We must find her again, that's all! And at once!

They disappear.

10

Courtroom. Groups: SHU FU *and* MRS. MI TZU; YANG SUN *and* MRS. YANG; WONG, *the* CARPENTER, *the* GRAND-FATHER, *the* NIECE, *the* OLD MAN, *the* OLD WOMAN; MRS. SHIN, *the* POLICEMAN; *the* UNEMPLOYED MAN, *the* SISTER-IN-LAW.

OLD MAN: So much power isn't good for one man.

UNEMPLOYED MAN: And he's going to open twelve super tobacco markets!

WIFE: One of the judges is a friend of Mr. Shu Fu's.

SISTER-IN-LAW: Another one accepted a present from Mr. Shui Ta only last night. A great fat goose.

OLD WOMAN (*to* WONG): And Shen Te is nowhere to be found.

WONG: Only the gods will ever know the truth.

POLICEMAN: Order in the court! My lords the judges!

Enter the THREE GODS *in judges' robes. We overhear their conversation as they pass along the footlights to their bench.*

THIRD GOD: We'll never get away with it, our certificates were so badly forged.

SECOND GOD: My predecessor's "sudden indigestion" will certainly cause comment.

FIRST GOD: But he *had* just eaten a whole goose.

UNEMPLOYED MAN: Look at that! *New* judges.

WONG: New judges. And what good ones!

> *The* THIRD GOD *hears this, and turns to smile at* WONG. *The* GODS *sit. The* FIRST GOD *beats on the bench with his gavel. The* POLICEMAN *brings in* SHUI TA *who walks with lordly steps. He is whistled at.*

POLICEMAN (*to* SHUI TA): Be prepared for a surprise. The judges have been changed.

> SHUI TA *turns quickly round, looks at them, and staggers.*

NIECE: What's the matter now?

WIFE: The great Tobacco King nearly fainted.

HUSBAND: Yes, as soon as he saw the new judges.

WONG: Does *he* know who they are?

> SHUI TA *picks himself up, and the proceedings open.*

FIRST GOD: Defendant Shui Ta, you are accused of doing away with your cousin Shen Te in order to take possession of her business. Do you plead guilty or not guilty?

SHUI TA: Not guilty, my lord.

FIRST GOD (*thumbing through the documents of the case*): The first witness is the policeman. I shall ask him to tell us something of the respective reputations of Miss Shen Te and Mr. Shui Ta.

POLICEMAN: Miss Shen Te was a young lady who aimed to please, my lord. She liked to live and let live, as the saying goes. Mr. Shui Ta, on the other hand, is a man of principle. Though the generosity of Miss Shen Te forced him at times to abandon half measures, unlike the girl he was always on the side of the law, my lord. One time, he even unmasked a gang of thieves to whom his too trustful cousin had given shelter. The evidence, in short, my lord, proves that Mr. Shui Ta was *incapable* of the crime of which he stands accused!

FIRST GOD: I see. And are there others who could testify along, shall we say, the same lines?

SHU FU *rises.*

POLICEMAN (*whispering to* GODS): Mr. Shu Fu—a very important person.

FIRST GOD (*inviting him to speak*): Mr. Shu Fu!

SHU FU: Mr. Shui Ta is a businessman, my lord. Need I say more?

FIRST GOD: Yes.

SHU FU: Very well, I will. He is Vice President of the Council of Commerce and is about to be elected a Justice of the Peace. (*He returns to his seat.*)

MRS. MI TZU *rises.*

WONG: Elected! *He* gave him the job!

With a gesture the FIRST GOD *asks who* MRS. MI TZU *is.*

POLICEMAN: Another very important person. Mrs. Mi Tzu.

MRS. MI TZU: My lord, as Chairman of the Committee on Social Work, I wish to call attention to just a couple of eloquent facts: Mr. Shui Ta not only has erected a model factory with model housing in our city, he is a regular contributor to our home for the disabled. (*She returns to her seat.*)

POLICEMAN (*whispering*): And she's a great friend of the judge that ate the goose!

FIRST GOD (*to the* POLICEMAN): Oh, thank you. What next? (*To the Court, genially:*) Oh, yes. We should find out if any of the evidence is less favorable to the defendant.

WONG, *the* CARPENTER, *the* OLD MAN, *the* OLD WOMAN, *the* UNEMPLOYED MAN, *the* SISTER-IN-LAW, *and the* NIECE *come forward.*

POLICEMAN (*whispering*): Just the riffraff, my lord.

FIRST GOD (*addressing the "riffraff"*). Well, um, riffraff— do you know anything of the defendant, Mr. Shui Ta?

WONG: Too much, my lord.

UNEMPLOYED MAN: What don't we know, my lord.

CARPENTER: He ruined us.

SISTER-IN-LAW: He's a cheat.

NIECE: Liar.

WIFE: Thief.

BOY: Blackmailer.

BROTHER: Murderer.

FIRST GOD: Thank you. We should now let the defendant state his point of view.

SHUI TA: I only came on the scene when Shen Te was in danger of losing what I had understood was a gift from the gods. Because I did the filthy jobs which someone had to do, they hate me. My activities were restricted to the minimum, my lord.

SISTER-IN-LAW: He had us arrested!

SHUI TA: Certainly. You stole from the bakery!

SISTER-IN-LAW: Such concern for the bakery! You didn't want the shop for yourself, I suppose!

SHUI TA: I didn't want the shop overrun with parasites.

SISTER-IN-LAW: We had nowhere else to go.

SHUI TA: There were too many of you.

WONG: What about this old couple: Were *they* parasites?

OLD MAN: We lost our shop because of you!

OLD WOMAN: And we gave your cousin money!

SHUI TA: My cousin's fiancé was a flyer. The money had to go to *him*.

WONG: Did you care whether he flew or not? Did you care whether she married him or not? You wanted her to marry someone else! (*He points at* SHU FU.)

SHUI TA: The flyer unexpectedly turned out to be a scoundrel.

YANG SUN (*jumping up*): Which was the reason you made him your manager?

SHUI TA: Later on he improved.

WONG: And when he improved, you sold him to her? (*He points out* MRS. MI TZU.)

SHUI TA: She wouldn't let me have her premises unless she had him to stroke her knees!

MRS. MI TZU: What? The man's a pathological liar. (*To him*:) Don't mention my property to me as long as you live! Murderer! (*She rustles off, in high dudgeon.*)

YANG SUN (*pushing in*): My lord, I wish to speak for the defendant.

SISTER-IN-LAW: Naturally. He's your employer.

UNEMPLOYED MAN: And the worst slave driver in the country.

MRS. YANG: That's a lie! My lord, Mr. Shui Ta is a great man. He . . .

YANG SUN: He's this and he's that, but he is not a murderer, my lord. Just fifteen minutes before his arrest I heard Shen Te's voice in his own back room.

FIRST GOD: Oh? Tell us more!

YANG SUN: I heard sobbing, my lord!

FIRST GOD: But lots of women sob, we've been finding.

YANG SUN: Could I fail to recognize her voice?

SHU FU: No, you made her sob so often yourself, young man!

YANG SUN: Yes. But I also made her happy. Till he (*pointing at* SHUI TA) decided to sell her to you!

SHUI TA: Because you didn't love her.

WONG: Oh, no: it was for the money, my lord!

SHUI TA: And what was the money for, my lord? For the poor! And for Shen Te so she could go on being good!

WONG: For the poor? That he sent to his sweatshops? And why didn't you let Shen Te be good when you signed the big check?

SHUI TA: For the child's sake, my lord.

CARPENTER: What about *my* children? What did he do about them?

SHUI TA *is silent.*

WONG: The shop was to be a fountain of goodness. That was the gods' idea. You came and spoiled it!

SHUI TA: If I hadn't, it would have run dry!

MRS. SHIN: There's a lot in that, my lord.

WONG: What have you done with the good Shen Te, bad

man? She *was* good, my lords, she was, I swear it! (*He raises his hand in an oath.*)

THIRD GOD: What's happened to your hand, water seller?

WONG (*pointing to* SHUI TA): It's all his fault, my lord, *she* was going to send me to a doctor—(*To* SHUI TA:) You were her worst enemy!

SHUI TA: I was her only friend!

WONG: Where is she then? Tell us where your good friend is!

The excitement of this exchange has run through the whole crowd.

ALL: Yes, where is she? Where is Shen Te? (*Etc.*)

SHUI TA: Shen Te . . . had to go.

WONG: Where? Where to?

SHUI TA: I cannot tell you! I cannot tell you!

ALL: Why? Why did she have to go away? (*Etc.*)

WONG (*into the din with the first words, but talking on beyond the others*): Why not, why not? Why did she have to go away?

SHUI TA (*shouting*): Because you'd all have torn her to shreds, that's why! My lords, I have a request. Clear the court! When only the judges remain, I will make a confession.

ALL (*except* WONG, *who is silent, struck by the new turn of events*): So he's guilty? He's confessing! (*Etc.*)

FIRST GOD (*using the gavel*): Clear the court!

POLICEMAN: Clear the court!

WONG: Mr. Shui Ta has met his match this time.

MRS. SHIN (*with a gesture toward the judges*): You're in for a little surprise.

The court is cleared. Silence.

SHUI TA: Illustrious ones!

The GODS *look at each other, not quite believing their ears.*

SHUI TA: Yes, I recognize you!

SECOND GOD (*taking matters in hand, sternly*): What have you done with our good woman of Setzuan?

SHUI TA: I have a terrible confession to make: I am she! (*He takes off his mask, and tears away his clothes.* SHEN TE *stands there.*)

SECOND GOD: Shen Te!

SHEN TE: Shen Te, yes. Shui Ta *and* Shen Te. Both.

Your injunction
To be good and yet to live
Was a thunderbolt:
It has torn me in two
I can't tell how it was
But to be good to others
And myself at the same time
I could not do it

Your world is not an easy one, illustrious ones!
When we extend our hand to a begger, he tears it off
    for us
When we help the lost, we are lost ourselves
And so
Since not to eat is to die
Who can long refuse to be bad?
As I lay prostrate beneath the weight of good
    intentions
Ruin stared me in the face
It was when I was unjust that I ate good meat
And hobnobbed with the mighty
Why?
Why are bad deeds rewarded?
Good ones punished?
I enjoyed giving
I truly wished to be the Angel of the Slums
But washed by a foster mother in the water of the
    gutter
I developed a sharp eye
The time came when pity was a thorn in my side
And, later, when kind words turned to ashes in my
    mouth
And anger took over
I became a wolf
Find me guilty, then, illustrious ones,
But know:
All that I have done I did
To help my neighbor
To love my lover
And to keep my little one from want
For your great, godly deeds, I was too poor, too small.

Pause.

FIRST GOD (*shocked*): Don't go on making yourself miser-
    able, Shen Te! We're overjoyed to have found you!

SHEN TE: I'm telling you I'm the bad man who committed all those crimes!

FIRST GOD (*using—or failing to use—his ear trumpet*): The good woman who did all those good deeds?

SHEN TE: Yes, but the bad man too!

FIRST GOD (*as if something had dawned*): Unfortunate coincidences! Heartless neighbors!

THIRD GOD (*shouting in his ear*): But how is she to continue?

FIRST GOD: Continue? Well, she's a strong, healthy girl . . .

SECOND GOD: You didn't hear what she said!

FIRST GOD: I heard every word! She is confused, that's all! (*He begins to bluster.*) And what about this book of rules—we can't renounce our rules, can we? (*More quietly.*) Should the world be changed? How? By whom? The world should *not* be changed! (*At a sign from him, the lights turn pink, and music plays.*)*

And now the hour of parting is at hand.
Dost thou behold, Shen Te, yon fleecy cloud?
It is our chariot. At a sign from me
'Twill come and take us back from whence we came
Above the azure vault and silver stars. . . .

SHEN TE: No! Don't go, illustrious ones!

---

* The rest of this scene has been adapted for the many American theatres that do not have "fly-space" to lower things from ropes. The translation in the first Minnesota edition, following the German exactly, is reprinted here on pages 142-144.—E. B.

FIRST GOD:

> Our cloud has landed now in yonder field
> From which it will transport us back to heaven.
> Farewell, Shen Te, let not thy courage fail thee. . . .

Exeunt GODS.

SHEN TE: What about the old couple? They've lost their shop! What about the water seller and his hand? And I've got to defend myself against the barber, because I don't love him! And against Sun, because I do love him! How? How?

SHEN TE's eyes follow the GODS *as they are imagined to step into a cloud which rises and moves forward over the orchestra and up beyond the balcony.*

FIRST GOD (*from on high*): We have faith in you, Shen Te!

SHEN TE: There'll be a child. And he'll have to be fed. I can't stay here. Where shall I go?

FIRST GOD: Continue to be good, good woman of Setzuan!

SHEN TE: I need my bad cousin!

FIRST GOD: But not very often!

SHEN TE: Once a week at least!

FIRST GOD: Once a month will be quite enough!

SHEN TE (*shrieking*): No, no! Help!

But the cloud continues to recede as the GODS *sing.*

VALEDICTORY HYMN

What rapture, oh, it is to know
    A good thing when you see it
And having seen a good thing, oh,
    What rapture 'tis to flee it

Be good, sweet maid of Setzuan
    Let Shui Ta be clever
Departing, we forget the man
    Remember your endeavor

Because through all the length of days
    Her goodness faileth never
    Sing hallelujah! Make Shen Te's
    Good name live on forever!

SHEN TE: Help!

EPILOGUE

You're thinking, aren't you, that this is no right
Conclusion to the play you've seen tonight?*
After a tale, exotic, fabulous,
A nasty ending was slipped up on us.
We feel deflated too. We too are nettled
To see the curtain down and nothing settled.
How could a better ending be arranged?
Could one change people? Can the world be changed?
Would new gods do the trick? Will atheism?
Moral rearmament? Materialism?
It is for you to find a way, my friends,
To help good men arrive at happy ends.
You write the happy ending to the play!
There must, there must, there's got to be a way!†

---

* *At afternoon performances:*
  We quite agree, our play this afternoon
  Collapsed upon us like a pricked balloon.
† When I first received the German manuscript of *Good
Woman* from Brecht in 1945 it had no Epilogue. He wrote it
a little later, influenced by misunderstandings of the ending in
the press on the occasion of the Viennese première of the play.
I believe that the Epilogue has sometimes been spoken by the
actress playing Shen Te, but the actor playing Wong might be
a shrewder choice, since the audience has already accepted him
as a kind of chorus. On the other hand, it is not *Wong* who
should deliver the Epilogue: whichever actor delivers it should
drop the character he has been playing.—E. B.

ALTERNATE ENDING FOR
GERMAN PRODUCTION

FIRST GOD:

> And now . . . (*He makes a sign and music is heard.
> Rosy light.*) let us return.
> This little world has much engaged us.
> Its joy and its sorrow have refreshed and pained us.
> Up there, however, beyond the stars,
> We shall gladly think of you, Shen Te, the good
> woman
> Who bears witness to our spirit down below,
> Who, in cold darkness, carries a little lamp!
> Good-bye! Do it well!

> *He makes a sign and the ceiling opens. A pink cloud
> comes down. On it the* THREE GODS *rise, very slowly.*

SHEN TE: Oh, don't, illustrious ones! Don't go away! Don't
leave me! How can I face the good old couple who've
lost their store and the water seller with his stiff hand?
And how can I defend myself from the barber whom
I do not love and from Sun whom I do love? And
I am with child. Soon there'll be a little son who'll
want to eat. I can't stay here! (*She turns with a
hunted look toward the door which will let her
tormentors in.*)

FIRST GOD: You can do it. Just be good and everything
will turn out well!

Enter the witnesses. They look with surprise at the judges floating on their pink cloud.

WONG: Show respect! The gods have appeared among us! Three of the highest gods have come to Setzuan to find a good human being. They had found one already, but . . .

FIRST GOD: No "but"! Here she is!

ALL: Shen Te!

FIRST GOD: She has not perished. She was only hidden. She will stay with you. A good human being!

SHEN TE: But I need my cousin!

FIRST GOD: Not too often!

SHEN TE: At least once a week!

FIRST GOD: Once a month. That's enough!

SHEN TE: Oh, don't go away, illustrious ones! I haven't told you everything! I need you desperately!

The GODS sing.

THE TRIO OF THE VANISHING GODS ON THE CLOUD

Unhappily we cannot stay
More than a fleeting year.
If we watch our find too long
It will disappear.

Here the golden light of truth
With shadow is alloyed

Therefore now we ask your leave
To go back to our void.

SHEN TE: Help! (*Her cries continue through the song.*)

Since our search is over now
Let us fast ascend!
The good woman of Setzuan
Praise we at the end!

As SHEN TE *stretches out her arms to them in desperation, they disappear above, smiling and waving.*